I Got There

I Got There

How a Mixed-Race Kid Overcame Racism, Poverty, and Abuse to Arrive at the American Dream

JeVon McCormick

PRESIDENT AND CEO OF SCRIBE MEDIA

LIONCREST
PUBLISHING

I GOT THERE
How a Mixed-Race Kid Overcame Racism, Poverty,
and Abuse to Arrive at the American Dream

SECOND EDITION

ISBN   978-1-61961-556-4   *Hardcover*
       978-1-61961-558-8   *Ebook*

PUBLISHER'S CATALOGING-IN-PUBLICATION DATA
Name: McCormick, J.T., author.

Title: I got there : how a mixed-race kid overcame racism , poverty ,
and abuse to arrive at the American Dream / J.T. McCormick.

Description: Austin, TX: Lioncrest Publishing, 2018.

Identifiers: ISBN 978-1-61961-556-4 (Hardcover) | 978-1-61961-557-1
(pbk.) | 978-1-61961-558-8 (ebook) | LCCN 2018946261

Subjects: LCSH McCormick, J.T. | Businesspeople--United
States--Biography. | African-American businesspeople--United
States--Biography. | African-Americans--Biography. | Businessmen--
United States--Biography. | Success in Business. | Entrepreneurship.
| Racism--United States--Anecdotes. | BISAC BIOGRAPHY
& AUTOBIOGRAPHY / Personal Memoirs | BIOGRAPHY &
AUTOBIOGRAPHY / Business | BIOGRAPHY & AUTOBIOGRAPHY
/ Cultural, Ethnic & Regional / African American & Black.

Classification: LCC HC102.5.A2 M343 2018 | DDC 338/.76/092--dc23

To my mom, Anna: There are no words that can express how I feel, and I'll always thank the Lord you made me.

All my childhood memories are full of all the sweet things you did for me. I appreciate how you raised me and all the extra love that you gave me.

When I was sick as a little kid, to keep me happy, there were no limits to the things you did.

I finally understand, for a woman, it ain't easy trying to raise a man. You were always committed. A poor single mother on welfare—no clue how you did it.

There's NO way I can pay you back, and I'll never fully understand, but I want you to know YOU raised a good man.

I love you, Mom. You are appreciated.

To my wife, Megan, who's always accepted me for me and supported my hustle, drive, and ambition: you are and always will be my perfect wife and mother to our children.

To my children, Danielle, Ava, Jaxon, Elle, and Jace, *and to my great-great-great-great-grandchildren whom I will never have the pleasure of meeting: I want you to know where you came from.*

Contents

————

Preface

___

WHILE THE OVERALL MESSAGE OF THIS BOOK IS OPTIMISTIC and positive, many of the details of my past are not.

This book contains true stories about physical and sexual abuse, racism, violence, and other unpleasant adult situations. None of it is gratuitous, but at times, I do speak directly and plainly, and there is strong language used.

I want to warn you about this and apologize up front. None of the stories or the language I've included is meant to offend anyone.

I left the adult situations and hard language in because it's what happened to me. This book is meant to show my family where I came from and to help others who've had difficult experiences deal with their past—especially those men and women who come from where I came from.

That means I have to tell the truth, the whole truth, about our world.

From Nothing to CEO

———

I'VE SPENT MY WHOLE LIFE RUNNING FROM THIS PLACE, and now here I am, back again.

Except this time, it's totally different. Instead of sitting with them, I was on stage, speaking to them.

I stood in front of the microphone. Before I said a word, I casually flicked my arms up from my side and rolled up the sleeves of my shirt. I took my time with my left sleeve, making sure my watch caught the sunlight.

Not only did I want my audience to wait for me, but I also wanted them to see what I had on. My custom-tailored three-piece suit, my perfectly creased pants, my leather shoes, and most importantly, my very large and very expensive gold watch.

Even though this was a captive audience, I was going to have to work very hard for their attention. I've spoken in front of much larger crowds and delivered speeches that mattered more (at least in business), but this was the most nervous I'd ever been.

Everything—their futures and my relationship to my past—hinged on my getting through to them.

I started by answering the unstated question:

"I'm not a drug dealer.

I'm not a rapper.

I'm not an athlete.

But I am very successful."

That's not how you're supposed to open a speech if you're a successful businessman, especially if you're a successful minority businessman in America.

But I'm no ordinary businessman, and this was no ordinary speech.

> *"I've made millions of dollars. I'm currently the president of a multimillion-dollar company that has offices in four cities and over one hundred employees.*
>
> *That's right. I'm wealthy, powerful, and important.*
>
> *But I didn't start here.*
>
> *I came from where you came from. I started where you are. In a place just like this."*

They looked at me with a mixture of curiosity, awe, and a little skepticism. I relaxed a little. They were hooked.

The reason this childish power display worked is because the audience were *literally* children.

They ranged in ages from fifteen to seventeen. By acting like this—garishly asserting status markers they understood and respected, like money and expensive watches—they knew I wasn't some out-of-touch adult there to wag my finger and lecture them.

I was speaking their language.

"I know what your life has been like because I lived it. I'll give you an example:

How many of you ever been so hungry you picked the food out of the trash cans at school to take home with you because you knew there'd be nothing in the fridge when you got home? Raise your hands.

How many of you have seen your dad, or another man, beat your mom? Or your dad beat other women besides your mom? Raise your hands again."

I scanned the crowd. Everyone had their arms up.

These were not just any children. This was the graduating class of twenty-five males in a juvenile detention center.

Most of these boys had committed several serious crimes, and many would never leave the prison system, not in any real way.

I paused to really take in this scene.

How did I, a poor kid from the hood of Dayton, Ohio, get to a position in life where I was giving such a personal speech to this crowd?

I thought about the long, strange road that brought me here, to this stage. I came from the same streets they did and grew up in the same hard lifestyle—abuse, neglect, racism, and poverty. I even knew a life of petty crime, which put me in juvie several times.

> *"That's right. All of you have been through that, just like me. We've lived through hunger, through violence, and through abuse. I can't tell you how many times I saw my dad commit violence, especially against women.*
>
> *I saw my dad sell drugs, probably like many of you. I saw him pimp women. I saw crime all around me growing up. That used to be my life, just like it's yours now.*
>
> *Lemme tell you some stories of my life, before I became successful."*

As I told the details of my childhood to those boys and their families, the memories came back to me. Vivid.

The time my dad stopped in the middle of the highway and beat a girlfriend in the road.

The time I slept at a bus stop because I had nowhere else to go.

The time my dad took me from my mom without telling her and then abandoned me to people who beat and neglected me.

These were memories I'd put away in a deep place and tried to forget about. But for the sake of those boys, I was willing to dig them out.

> "I know people tell you to straighten up, to not live a life of crime. And I bet you think that's bullshit, don't you? You probably thought to yourself, What other option do I have? What else am I even good for?
>
> I thought that, too. When I was in juvie, I thought I had no other options either. One time, I was in juvie for two months because no one in my family knew where I was.
>
> There was a time in my life, when I was around your ages, when I thought no one cared about me. I figured since I was obviously worthless, why not steal stuff and be a criminal? I mean, I was going to die by the age of twenty-five anyway, so what did it matter?
>
> Does any of this sound familiar?"

Even though this was a serious juvenile detention center, it was not adult prison. It was still early enough in their lives for things to change. There was time for them.

That's why I was there. To give them the help I never got. To show them there was another way.

But it wasn't just about them. Giving this speech was as much about helping myself get past all of that awful history as it was helping these boys who were still going through it. If I wanted to heal my past, I couldn't do it alone.

> *"You don't have to be a drug dealer, or a rapper, or an athlete to make money and get out of the hood. And you definitely don't have to be a criminal and end up in prison or dead.*
>
> *There is another path for you—the path I took.*
>
> *And you know where my path to making millions of dollars and achieving business success started? It started by cleaning toilets at a restaurant.*
>
> *No one scrubs porcelain better than me! You think I'm fucking with you, but to this day, I'm still proud of that! My toilets in that Po' Folks Restaurant sparkled!*
>
> *And let me tell you, you think hustling only works on the streets? Bullshit. I'm here, on this stage, because I never stopped hustling. I just adapted my hustle to make it legal.*
>
> *In fact, here's what they don't tell you—the corporate world*

loves hustling. They just have another name for it. They call it 'sales.'

I'll give you an example. How many of you have sold drugs? If you can sling dope, you can sell the hell outta legal drugs. They're called pharmaceuticals, and the people who sell those get PAID.

If you can survive in here, you can thrive in that world. If you can survive in juvie, then working your way through the business world is easy.

I know this is true because I did it. And if I can do it, so can you.

I won't bullshit you. It's a helluva lot harder to succeed coming from where we come from than coming from the suburbs. They have a lot of advantages that we don't have.

But it IS possible for you to have the life I have. You can even go further than me. And I'm going to tell you how to get there."

The boys' eyes were wide, mouths dropped open in an O as they listened to me.

My anxiety was gone. Now I was excited. I was getting through to them.

I knew what they were thinking, because it's what I would have thought if I'd seen someone like myself while I was in juvenile detention: *I can get out of this and get what he has? For real? Where do I sign up?!?!*

No one had ever told them there was a way out, just like no one had told me. I could see the effect on them—the hope in their eyes—and it energized me. It carried me through the rest of the speech as I outlined the path these boys needed to take and how they could get the help they needed to get to where I was or further.

When I finished my speech, I got a standing ovation. I was elated.

I stayed around and spoke to many of the family members who had come. This might sound weird, but even though I didn't know these people before the speech, I felt like a conquering hero returning home from a long journey. All the nervousness was gone, and what was left was release and joy. Not just that I had crushed it in that speech, but that it really seemed to get through to the kids and the families.

I have to be honest: for a moment, I lost myself in the praise. There was still plenty of work to be done, but I felt like a bridge had been built. A bridge of belief, a bridge that could take them from despair to success.

Then it all flipped. A grandmother approached me and said, "I wish my grandson would have heard this ten years ago."

"Ten years ago?" I asked her.

"He's seventeen now," she told me. "He's been in and out of juvenile since he was seven years old. He's in for murder. I worry it's too late for him."

A chill ran through me. She told me his story, and it was heartbreaking.

What do you even say to that? How do you respond to a seven-year-old—a child who should be climbing on monkey bars, swinging a baseball bat, or riding his bike—locked behind bars because he's busy committing crimes? And that kid eventually killed someone?

That ended my joy. That conversation remains seared into my mind and heart. I haven't been able to shake it. In fact, that conversation led directly to this book.

Looking back on it now, I think the reason this hit me so hard was because it was the first time I realized something I'd hid from my whole life—that seven-year-old could have been me.

In a way, that seven-year-old *was* me.

By the grace of God, I became the one on stage and not the one in for murder...and the sheer terror that I almost didn't make it out—and the shame and guilt that I did—has driven me every day since.

ONE

My Family

———

"COME ON, JEVON, LET'S GET YOU DRESSED," MOM shouted. "Your dad called. He's on his way to pick you up."

Grinning, I sprinted to my room. I pulled on my jeans, yanked a clean shirt over my head, put on a clean pair of socks, and slid my feet into my beat-up sneakers.

With a fresh set of clothes on, I raced to the windowsill and scrambled on top of the electric heater. It gave me the extra height I needed so I could place my hands on the window frame and peer through the glass. We lived in a tiny apartment, a few stories above the street; it was the perfect height to watch for my dad's car. I swiveled my head back and forth, waiting and watching.

I was excited to see my dad. His visits were rare. He'd swing by for me once, maybe twice a month. If I saw him three times, well, that was incredible. I knew the moment I saw his car what I would do. It was always the same routine. First, I'd wait for him to park the car. Then I'd jump from the heater, spring to the door, and race down the stairs. Once at the bottom, I'd yank open the apartment door, run toward him, and then launch myself into his arms. Dad would catch me, then throw me high into the air, finally swinging me around in a circle. This was our thing, and I loved it.

"Mom, there he is!" I jammed my finger into the glass, shouting to my mom who stood silently behind me.

"Oh, no, that's not him," I muttered, disappointed when the car sped past. My excitement quickly returned as I continued watching and waiting for my father. More cars drove by. People strolled down the street.

"Oh, there he is!" I cried again; except, again, I was wrong. It wasn't Dad, just another car that looked like my father's.

Hours passed.

"Why don't you go outside and play, JeVon?" Mom asked.

"No, no, I don't want to miss him when he gets here," I

replied, shaking my head and without taking my eyes off the street.

I stood on that electric heater peering into the world below for four or five hours. It wasn't the first time and it wouldn't be the last time I stood waiting for him at the window.

I stood on the electric heater and stared out the window until my eyelids grew heavy. I rested my forehead against the windowpane, trying in vain to give my small frame extra support.

The next thing that I remember was waking up on the couch. Rubbing my eyes with my tiny fists, I rolled over.

"I'm so sorry, JeVon," Mom said as she rubbed circles on my back. "Your dad came when you were asleep."

I couldn't hide my disappointment.

"But he left this for you," she said with a smile as she handed me a Hot Wheels toy.

I reached for the toy and twisted it in my hands. I liked getting a toy, but it wasn't the same as a visit with my dad. Learning that he had come when I fell asleep hurt.

I was upset and mad, mostly at myself, believing that it was my fault that I'd missed him. *If only I hadn't fallen asleep, then I could have gone with Dad*, I thought.

This scene happened to me a lot. Dad would call and tell Mom that he was coming to get me. I'd stand for hours at the window, waiting for him, only to fall asleep. Without fail, I'd promise myself that the next time he was coming for me, I'd do better at staying awake.

So the next time would come, and I'd stand at the window-sill longer than the last time. *Nothing will move or cause me to miss my dad again*, I'd think. But my small body would fail me every time, and eventually, I'd fall asleep. When I awoke from my deep slumber, there, next to me, would be a Hot Wheels car, a small book, or another inexpensive toy.

I'd think that even though my dad was late again, and I'd fallen asleep again, at least he'd bought me a toy. At least he thought about me.

No, the toy didn't make up for missing an outing with my dad, but I'd still run outside with my toy to show the other neighborhood kids. I'd always brag about my dad, about what he'd bought me and how great he was. Most of us lived without our fathers, and some had no idea who their fathers were. But I knew mine, and mine came to take me out and bought me toys. Maybe he only offered me crumbs, but those were crumbs I gladly devoured. They were crumbs none of the other boys received. Crumbs were better than nothing.

I was in my thirties when my mom told me the truth about the toys.

My father had never left them because he'd never showed. It was my mom who'd left those gifts for me, wanting to protect me from the pain of feeling rejected and ignored by my dad.

When I learned the truth, I was livid. She led me to believe my father was someone he wasn't. It hurt learning none of it was real, and I hated knowing that I had boasted about my father to other kids, especially because those kids were just as starved for their own fathers' affections.

"You won't understand why I did this until you have children of your own one day, JeVon," Mom said. "When you have your own children, you'll do whatever it takes to make your children happy."

I don't think I spoke to my mom for almost three months after her confession.

I was so angry because I had been so happy that my dad

showed up and so proud that he cared about me, but it wasn't him. I think I was mad because I had given him so much love then, when it wasn't him who deserved it. It was her.

Now, years later and the father of five beautiful children, I understand what she meant when she said you'll do whatever it takes to make your children happy. If I need to wear a pink tutu and some tights to cheer up my daughter and make her smile, then I'll be rocking that outfit. I wouldn't care what anyone thought.

Mom was right. I'd do whatever I had to do to make my children happy.

My father's missed visits taught me an invaluable lesson: to *always* keep my word. To this day, I have an unwavering commitment to do what I say I will do. It's part of what has helped to fuel my business success. Everyone knows that if I say I will do something, then I'll follow through.

I am so emphatic about this because I never want to be the type of person who inflicts this kind of pain on anyone. I remember what it feels like. The pain, the agony, the deep hurt that comes from anticipating your father, and then he doesn't come. I refuse to do that to anyone else.

Of course, I'm always there for my kids; but in my life now, it extends far beyond that. And even beyond keeping my word in business.

In fact, when I schedule time at the halfway house or the juvenile detention centers I volunteer at, I lock it in. No meeting, no call, nothing can interrupt or alter that time.

Why? Because I won't be my dad. For many of these kids, I'm the closest thing to a father they have. And when I show up, they treat me like it; they're excited to tell me how they got a job, how they got a raise, or just to talk about any of the small positive changes they've experienced in their lives.

I can't change how my father treated me, but I can make sure I never act like him.

MY FATHER

My dad was the quintessential street hustler, part of the 1970s scene in Dayton. His life was straight out of a Hollywood movie about pimps and drug dealers. He had a stereotypical "pimp pad" and hung out with local funk groups, such as the Ohio Players, Slave, and Lakeside, who went on to fame. Dayton was the center of the funk scene in the 1970s. If you've seen the movie *American Gangster* (the one where Denzel Washington played Frank Lucas), that was how my dad dressed and acted. I love watching that movie because it reminds me of my dad.

Although I called him Dad, he didn't raise me. That responsibility was solely my mom's. Sure, he took me out a few times each month, but he wasn't a stable, positive influence who parented me. When I think of my dad, the words *unreliable* and *irresponsible* come to mind.

He was also the furthest thing from a "good guy," and no one would ever accuse him of being a family man. He fathered twenty-three children (who are confirmed) but never offered to pay child support for any of us. I was born in September. I have half brothers who were born in October and December of the same year, and a half sister who is not much younger than my mom.

During the 1970s, the car of choice for any black man, especially a pimp, was a Cadillac. My dad fit the part to a tee. He drove a red Cadillac Eldorado, with candy-apple red leather seats, red carpets, and a red exterior. He loved that car, and when he picked you up, you were barely allowed to breathe on the seats. You couldn't touch anything, and your feet had to stay on the carpets.

I remember one time when Dad was driving me, two of my half brothers, and one of his women. We had just left the fast-food place Wendy's, and the woman was holding a bag of burgers and fries in her lap. My dad and the woman started to argue. It got heated quickly (which wasn't a surprise).

Dad barreled down the four-lane highway, weaving in and out of traffic, and zipping by cars. As their voices rose, they started talking faster and faster, and got angrier and angrier. My eyes darted from the traffic outside my window to the front seat.

Suddenly, the paper bag crinkled as the woman reached inside, snatched a burger, and flung it as hard as she could at my father. The burger ricocheted off the side of his face and plopped onto the seat between them.

I held my breath and tried to keep from laughing as I thought, *Oh, damn! You got stuff on Dad's car? I can't believe you did that! That's game over!*

Recalling this memory, it's sad that what raced through my mind wasn't that the woman dared to throw something at my dad. No, it was that she dared to get my dad's red Cadillac Eldorado dirty by throwing a greasy hamburger at him. As I said, I don't think my dad loved anything more than he loved his car—not his kids and certainly not his women. Even more heartbreaking was that as a young kid, even I knew this truth about him.

My laughter disappeared when my father slammed on the brakes and jammed the gear stick into park in the middle of the lane on the busy highway.

My half brothers and I glanced at one another. I saw the same nervousness in their eyes that I felt in myself. We watched our father get out of the car, walk around to the passenger side, yank the door open, and drag the woman out of the car by her hair. He then beat her, Rodney King style, as cars whizzed by on the busy highway.

When he was done kicking and punching her, he grabbed her purse and dumped everything in it over her head. Then he reached back into the car and grabbed the bag of Wendy's and dumped the food on top of her, too.

Satisfied, he casually strolled back to his side of the car, slid behind the wheel, and popped the car into drive. As we drove away, leaving the woman crying in the middle of the highway, he glanced over his shoulder at the three of us.

"So, where do you boys want to go to eat?" he asked us, as if nothing had happened.

* * *

It seemed like everyone knew my father, especially in the neighborhoods where we hung out, where he did business, and where he'd take me for a drive. We couldn't go a block in his red Cadillac without someone waving, yelling, or blowing their horn at us. Not only did everyone know him, but they also seemed to love him.

On special days, I got to sit in the front with him. I'd watch as people would approach the car and my dad would roll down his window. They would bend down, drape their forearms across the open window so they could look eye to eye with my dad, and talk about whatever was on their mind.

I'd get mad at these interruptions because we were supposed to go somewhere, and he'd always get distracted. What should have been a fifteen-minute trip would turn into an hour. He stopped to talk to *everyone*. It was only later that I learned these conversations weren't all positive. Sometimes there was a drug deal going down or he was telling a woman to get back on the corner to make more money.

My father wasn't the type to sit down and teach me right from wrong or to have serious talks about how I should behave in the world. He didn't impart lessons to me, at least not directly. I learned by observing how my father navigated his world of illegal activity. I'd watch and listen, and then when I got older, I spun everything I learned into ways to help me advance but through legal means.

There was one teachable moment we had together that I'll never forget. His lesson? Always say "hi" to *everyone*. It's been an invaluable message that has served me well through the years. I just wish he had used a different means to teach me.

The lesson came one day when I was in the fourth grade. Dad had picked me up and I was spending the weekend with him. He brought me to the grocery store, and as we were walking down the frozen food aisle, a little girl walked by and said, "Hi, JeVon!"

Instead of responding, I put my head down and kept walking, pretending that she wasn't there or that I didn't hear her.

Whack! Tingles ran down the back of my neck as my father smacked me upside the head with an open palm. The force of his blow caused me to stumble, and I fell face first to the cold floor. My eyes watered, and blood dripped from my nose as my head bounced off the ground. Then Dad grabbed the back of my shirt, hauled me to my feet, and pinned me with his forearm under my chin against a freezer door.

"I don't care who it is, JeVon," he growled. "You say 'hi' to *everyone*. You say 'hi' to the janitor, you say 'hi' to the teacher, you say 'hi' to your friends," he spat.

I won't teach my kids the same way my father taught me, but my dad was right. Part of my success has come because I'm hypervigilant about saying hello to everyone, from the janitor to the waitress to the CEO. I acknowledge the work they're doing, and I treat them with respect. I've found that you can go much further in life when you genuinely ask someone how they are, and then listen for their response.

MY MOTHER

My mom grew up in an institutional orphanage that was more like a prison-style children's home during the 1950s and 1960s. She never knew her parents. She didn't know where she came from. She left the orphanage with a tattered, teal wooden suitcase that held all her clothes and possessions in this world. She was only in her late teens when she left the orphanage with her suitcase and twenty dollars in her pocket.

She and a friend found jobs selling encyclopedias door to door. As the story goes, one day they were taking a break at a bus stop when my dad drove by. He circled the block about three or four times, and on his last pass, he hollered out the window asking my mom if she wanted to grab something to eat.

I can only imagine what it must have been like for her,

catching my father's attention. Growing up isolated and alone, I imagine few people had shown her any attention. I imagine few people had been nice to her. Then this grown man, fifteen years older than her, pulled up in a flashy car, dressed in real nice clothes, and talked to her. My dad was always a smooth talker and a great conversationalist. I'm sure he knew exactly the right words to say to my mom. He was great at playing the game.

Apparently, my dad took my mom out, bought her something to eat, and that's it. I was born within a year of them meeting.

It took me more than thirty years before I had the courage to ask my mom if she was one of my dad's prostitutes. She said no. In fact, it was the reason my parents were together for only a couple of years and never married or lived together. When she first met him, she had no idea about his line of work. But when she learned the truth, she was out.

It's easy to see how my dad was likely grooming her to become one of his girls. Pimps like my father prey on the naïve, gullible ones—girls who may not have received much attention growing up or who were victims of abuse. Coming from the orphanage with no understanding of the world, and with no loving support system to help, it's understandable that my dad would target her.

Nevertheless, my mom walked away from my dad and his life. It took courage and strength for her to do what she did. To this day, I'm in awe of her for it.

Actually, I'm in awe of my mom for a lot of things. Take my last name, McCormick, for example. That's my mom's name, not my father's. Dad fathered twenty-three kids, and most of my half brothers and half sisters took his name.

I was rare.

My mom has no background and no idea where she came from. Even the name McCormick is a mystery. Did the orphanage pick it for her? Was she dropped off at the orphanage with that name? I don't know. I'll never know where my last name came from or even where my mother came from. She has no lineage, and as a result, I have no clue who my ancestors are either. I have no clue who my grandfather and grandmother are, or who my uncles and aunts, if I have any, are. I have no idea who my great-grandparents were, or what countries they came from.

This may not seem like a big deal, but imagine what it would be like to go to the doctor's office. When you fill out the stack of paperwork, inevitably you're asked about your family history. There are boxes to check if your family has a history of heart disease or cancer. I can't check those boxes because I have no idea.

When Mom left the orphanage, she left with few possessions. A raggedy suitcase, some clothes, and a few keepsakes were all she carried with her. When I was born, she had few material possessions to give to me, but the name McCormick was hers; that was something she could give to me. I'm forever grateful that she gave me her name, because she was my only parent. She raised me, she taught me right from wrong, she loved me, and she sheltered me.

I'm honored to carry her name, even if we have no idea where this Irish name came from. What matters to me is that it came from her.

* * *

My mom had no family when I was growing up. I was it. In a sense, I was like a real-life baby doll whom she coveted, protected, and cared for the best that she could.

My mom was five feet nine with jet-black hair that hung down to her butt and green eyes. And she was *very* white—like a sheet of paper, white. When I think back on my early years with my mom, what I remember is glowing warmth and her personality. She was always loving to me. She protected and sheltered me for the first nine years of my life, despite our struggles in poverty.

When we had to walk places, because we didn't have bus fare, she made it fun. We'd stroll by the Ohio River and I would skip stones into the water, and she'd make up silly games that made me laugh.

We'd go to the Dayton Art Institute that had a massive bronze lion statue out front. I'd scamper on its back and pretend to ride it. And she would take me to watch free plays in the park.

During the Christmas season, she would bring me to the annual holiday parade and to Rike's Department Store where I peered through the big front window at the Christmas displays. It was like a scene out of the famous holiday movie, *A Christmas Story.* I was like that kid Ralphie with my nose against the windowpane, staring at all the toys in Rike's Department Store that I would not be getting.

Mom did anything and everything she could to make me happy. She always made sure we had a Thanksgiving meal and a Christmas holiday. She would even forgo making the full rent payment for December, so I could have a taste of the holiday season like the other kids. She'd cut a deal with the landlord, such as agreeing to sweep the halls of the building or doing other odd jobs around the complex to make up for the missed payment.

Each year, we would have a tiny, three-foot, Charlie Brown-like Christmas tree. Mom would drape a white sheet over a table, and then she'd set the tree on top. The height of the table made our tree look bigger. We'd take our handful of decorations and place them one at a time onto a limb. The tiny limbs would droop with the weight of each ornament. Every ornament was like a light going on. "Wow, look at that!" I'd say in awe after we hung an ornament.

After each ornament was hung, one at a time, Mom and I would back away from the tree to stare at our masterpiece. We'd tilt our heads from side to side, eyeing the tree and the placement of each ornament. Each ornament had to be placed in the perfect position. Once we were happy with our handiwork, we'd grab another decoration, gently hang it on a new branch, then back away again. One year, we made popcorn strings to loop around the tree—I loved that.

Some years, Mom found a string of Christmas lights for us to tape on the border of a window. It was a short string, not long enough to make it around the whole window frame, and only half the lights worked. It was one of the saddest strings of lights you've ever seen.

When the lights were hung around the windowsill, Mom and I would go outside and stand in the chilly December night to gaze at our twinkling lights. In those days, I didn't care that we had a short string of lights that barely worked. To me, seeing our half-lit window with our tiny tree silhouetted was like watching Rockefeller Center. For a moment, staring in amazement at our version of Christmas, I thought people were going to come and ice skate in front of us. We proudly hung those lights up, and to me, they were the best set of lights ever.

My mom made Christmas time the best. She made it seem bigger than it really was. But then, that was Mom. She made everything seem bigger and better to me, bigger and better than the reality of our situation.

It wasn't until I was an adult and saw the size of most Christmas trees that I realized how small and sad our trees had been. When my little girl turned two, I went crazy spending money on outside lights for our home. I think I did this because all I could see was that tiny string of lights that barely worked.

My mom had a way of making me feel cared for, too, as though we lacked for nothing. I still wonder how she made magic out of our extreme poverty. We were so poor that, some weeks, my mom had only two dollars to get us through. That was money for bus fare *and* food. Other months, like around the holidays, she could barely pay our rent. I have a receipt from a landlord that shows she paid ten dollars toward our $150 monthly rent bill. Often, we couldn't afford new shoes, so ours were littered with holes. When it snowed, she put bread bags over our shoes to keep the water from soaking through.

We didn't have a car. We had to ride the bus everywhere. When I tell this story to most people, they don't understand the full impact. When you're used to having a car, the word *everywhere* doesn't compute. When we had to go somewhere, our only options were the bus or our feet. When we had to do laundry, we carted our dirty clothes in black Hefty lawn bags onto the bus to get to the laundromat. When we had to buy groceries, we rode the bus with our arms loaded with one or two bags of food. When my mom had to pay a bill, run errands, or pick up our food stamps, we had to ride the bus or walk.

Many times, we spent hours sitting at the bus stop in the cold rain and heavy snow waiting for the bus to come. Sometimes it was on time, sometimes it was late, and sometimes it drove by us as though we didn't exist.

To this day, the two things I will always have are a car and a washer and dryer. I refuse to go to the laundromat or to ride a bus again. My daughter is obsessed with the bus. She wants to ride the bus all the time, and I'm adamant that she won't get on one. I know for her it'll be fun; it's going for a ride. But it's only fun for her because we have two cars, and she doesn't have to depend on the bus to get around.

One of the first times my mother came to visit me after I had found success in business, I picked her up in my car. She mentioned how nice it was. "Yeah, it's a long way from us riding that bus, or sitting in the rain or snow waiting for it, or having to sit there when the bus drove by us without stopping," I replied. When I told her it cost me $100,000, she swore at me. I laughed. "Mom, I'm proud of this car because I never forget riding that bus."

I know I shouldn't talk about money like that, but I couldn't help it. People who think money isn't a proper conversation subject are the ones who've always had it. For those of us who came from nothing, it's a reminder of who we are, where we came from, and an appreciation of the struggle.

As an adult, I know what riding the bus meant: it meant we were poor. But as a kid, I didn't know what being poor meant because I didn't know anything different. There wasn't a point of reference for me.

It wasn't until I got into school that I started to understand how poor my mom and I were. Every year, I got free lunch, and with free lunch came a small carton of white milk. Like most kids, though, I wanted chocolate milk. Sadly, that cost an extra ten cents. A dime doesn't sound like much, but that was a dime Mom couldn't spare. I didn't have a lot of wants as a kid, but I wanted chocolate milk. I wanted what the other kids had. I wanted a chocolate milk so badly that I would try to sneak a chocolate milk onto my tray.

I'd walk up to the register hoping the lunch lady would look the other way and let me get my milk. But that never happened. The lunch lady caught me every time, and every time she wordlessly snatched the chocolate milk carton off my tray and replaced it with white milk.

If you open the refrigerator in my home now, you'll find three gallons of chocolate milk. My daughter loves chocolate milk, and she can open the door and pull it out whenever she wants it.

But that wasn't the case for me. Some days, when I opened the refrigerator door, there was nothing inside. No food, no condiments—it was bare. Mom and I had eaten everything, and there was no money left to fill it.

There were times we struggled to have enough money for toothpaste. When the toothpaste tube was empty, Mom would cut it down the middle, fold it open, and then wipe our toothbrushes along the sides to scoop up the remnants.

I like to joke we were so poor we couldn't afford the *o* and *r* in the word; we were just *po*.

The best proof of this is how I learned the months of the year. Most kids learn them by repetition or, like my little girl, by learning a song. That's not how I learned them. I learned the months based on the number of days they had. The ones that had fewer days I learned to like because those were the months we didn't have to stretch our welfare and food stamps. February was an awesome month. We had to make our food stamps last for only twenty-eight days, sometimes twenty-nine if it was a leap year.

I hated months like May or July. They lasted thirty-one days. Those were the months when we ran out of food stamps. That meant when I got home from school, I was almost guaranteed to find an empty fridge and no dinner. So while my classmates laughed and played outside at recess, I stayed in the cafeteria eating scraps of food off lunch trays and picking through trash cans to find half-eaten sandwiches. My goal was to eat as much as I could to fill my belly enough to make it through the night and until the next day at school. This strategy didn't work all that well.

Despite our money struggles, my early years with my mom were happier than not—all thanks to her boundless love. Love doesn't fill your stomach, but it can do almost everything else, and she loved me.

LIFE IN DAYTON

Dayton is a smaller version of Detroit. Once, it was prosperous, too. Big companies like Dayton Tires brought jobs to the community, but those jobs left as companies moved their offices to other cities. When companies left, the city went with them.

Growing up in the 1970s, the city was racially divided. In Dayton, there were no Latinos. You were either white or black. As a child of a white mother and a black father, I was mixed race, and it meant that I didn't fit in anywhere. The black people didn't like me because I was half white, and the white people didn't like me because I was half black. I was of both worlds and yet of neither.

I felt out of place at school and tormented by an identity crisis. Kids called me names like Oreo and zebra. It was just as hard with my own family members who would ask me, "JeVon, would you rather be white or black?" as if I had some choice in the matter. My race wasn't optional. I was who I was. I was half white and I was half black. I suffered from the most unusual form of racism—*no one wanted me around.*

I remember standing in a long line with my mother waiting to pick up our monthly allotment of food stamps. This isn't like today's system, where people get a debit card that they can swipe for groceries. This was old-school paper money that you handed to the grocery store cashier when it was time to purchase your food. People saw you. They knew right away if you were on the system, unlike today where the debit cards let everyone blend in. It was humiliating watching my mom try to discreetly hand over the food stamps, trying her best to hide that she needed help from the government to feed her son.

One time, when my mom and I were waiting for our food stamps, this lady glanced at me and turned to my mom. "Nigger lover," she muttered with disgust. I couldn't believe this woman! There she was, just as poor as we were. She stood in the same line, waiting for the same monthly food stamps, but somehow, for some reason, she thought she was better than us.

But, then, that was the attitude in Dayton. People didn't like me, and they didn't like my mom because she had a kid with a black man. Once, I remember coming home to our apartment to find all our stuff thrown on the curb.

"No nigger lovers can live in my apartment complex," the landlord told my mom. Of course, he rented to black people. It was the mixing of races that he didn't believe in.

There we sat on the curb, just me and Mom and our few possessions. We were alone. She had no family to fall back on, no sister to call and ask if we could crash with her for a night. She had no father to call to come pick us up. We had nowhere to go, no one to call, and no idea what to do next.

But like she always did, Mom figured it out. She had to. She picked herself up off the curb, told me to grab our stuff and her hand, and we started walking. I don't remember where we ended up, but I know she found us a place somewhere.

Crime and violence also plagued my early childhood years in Dayton. For a midsize city, Dayton was one of the most dangerous places to live (an unfortunate distinction the city still holds today).

It was around Thanksgiving, and most people in our apartment complex were gone, off visiting their families and friends. Because I was the only family my mom had, it was just the two of us celebrating the holiday together. Unbeknownst to us, the gentleman who lived on the basement floor was also home.

Bang! Bang!

My body shot up from my bed as I awoke, startled by the sound of gunshots in the middle of the night. My mom crept to the door and looked back at me. She commanded me to stay behind her. The chain lock on the door rattled as she cracked the door open and peeked into the hallway. She heard the man from the basement moaning and yelling for help. She grabbed the phone and called 911. The ambulance came and took him to the hospital. He had been shot in the back. Had my mom not called, he would have bled to death on the floor in the hallway.

* * *

As much as she could, my mom tried to shelter me from the pain, poverty, and hunger that we endured. She never wanted me to feel any of it, but there was no escape. Most of the time, she was brave and put on a smile for me, but then there were times when I saw her cry over how little we had and how much she struggled. She was frustrated and scared. It broke my heart to see her upset.

For better or worse, seeing how hard my mom struggled—alone—to make it, taught me that I could count on only a small number of people in my life. My attitude for a very long time was, *No one cares, so I have to do it myself.*

And for a long time, that was true.

When I went to school without a free lunch ticket, I didn't eat. No one gave me a free meal. When our heat was turned off because my mom couldn't pay the bill, no one was there to turn it back on. If my mom had to work a job under the table to scrape together some pennies and dollars to get the heat turned back on, no one cared.

When my mom went to the dry cleaner and begged them to give us plastic so she could tape it over the windows of our fifth-floor apartment because the wind was so bad we froze, no one cared. When I had to put water on my cereal because we didn't have milk, no one cared. When my mom put bread bags on her feet because her shoes had holes in them and there was heavy snow on the ground, no one came to give my mom a free pair of shoes.

I saw all of this and I realized the world didn't care that we suffered.

Even today, although I know people have good hearts and they want to collaborate and work together with me, there's still a part of me that walks around believing that no one *really* cares about me and that I have to do everything for myself.

I know this mentality isn't healthy, and I realize it's a product of my environment. That's why it's important for me that when I throw my two-year-old daughter or one-year-old son into the air, I always reassure them, "Daddy's never going to drop you. Daddy's always going to take care of you."

I think a big part of the reason I say it so much is because of where I came from. I can't totally forget what it used to be like.

* * *

My father did little for me, but he indirectly showed me how things can be different when money lines your pockets. With my mom, we were just poor. But things with my dad were different. He was always immaculately dressed. He looked sharp. He'd pick me up in a new Cadillac. He'd take me to his well-furnished apartment.

With my dad, I saw what money did for a person. I saw how it could change your life. Money was the key; it was the driver not only of success but of safety, peace of mind, and happiness. I learned early in my life that if I could earn money, then everything in my life could be different.

We hear this a lot today, the notion that money doesn't buy happiness. I've been on both sides of this equation. I've been hungry, dirty, and dead broke, *and* I've made millions of dollars. It's true that money doesn't solve all your problems, but without a doubt, I would rather be rich and miserable than poor and miserable. At least rich and miserable means you aren't hungry or cold. No, money may not buy happiness, but being broke damn sure doesn't get you anything.

As best as she could, my mom sheltered me from the harsh reality of the world, trying with all her might to give me a loving sanctuary—whether that was lying to me about my father leaving me toys, taking on extra jobs over the Christmas holiday so I could have a tiny tree, or taking me to the free plays in the park so I could laugh.

For the first nine years of my life, she succeeded. My fondest memories of those years were with my mom—all that she did for me and all that we did together. My mom was (and still is today) a beautiful, wonderful woman who made the best out of a horrible situation. She was phenomenal. No, we didn't have a lot of money, but she loved me like no other. She made everything—every holiday, every trip to the grocery store, every walk by the river—bigger and better.

When I think back on those years, the first nine of my life, what I remember is my mom's love. I remember her protection. I remember her shelter. I remember how she always hugged me, kissed me good night, and told me that she loved me.

Unfortunately, even her love and devotion to me couldn't protect me forever.

TWO

Houston

———

MY DAD LIVED IN A "PIMP LAIR." HIS APARTMENT WALLS
were lined with bamboo, real lion and zebra skin rugs
lay scattered on the floor, and huge ivory tusks greeted
you when you walked through the front door. And then
there was the African art strewn throughout his jun-
gle-themed pad.

Sometimes I'd stay with my dad for a night or two on the
weekend. Occasionally, one or more of my half brothers
or half sisters would be there, too. One night, my dad had
me, one of my brothers, and one of his prostitutes at his
apartment. My brother and I were playing when we heard
a knock on the door.

"Come over here and hide," Dad hissed to us.

We hurried into the kitchen, but being nosy eight- and nine-year-olds, we peeked around the corner. A man, whom we had never seen before, walked in and went over to the prostitute, who then led him into the bedroom.

When we heard the bedroom door click shut, we sneaked out of the kitchen.

"Who's that man?" I asked my dad.

Dad looked at me and paused. "He's the insurance man."

I knew he wasn't telling me the truth, but at the time, I had no idea what he meant. I didn't understand pimps and prostitutes. Looking back now, my dad's response makes me laugh. He could have made up any story, given that man any title, but he called him the insurance man.

In a strange way, Dad was right. The man was insurance for him. He ensured that my father was paid and that he had a source of income. He ensured Dad drove a fancy car and wore fine clothes.

This moment stayed with me throughout my teenage and adult years. And looking back, it was one of the first times when I started to see parallels between the legal and illegal worlds. Both worlds had their own versions of an insurance man. When I got older, it was just another piece of the puzzle that showed me life was a game to be played, and the lessons of the street were just as relevant in the legal world.

* * *

Another time, I was at my dad's house with two half brothers, and we were playing Monopoly. Suddenly, the windows shattered, startling me and two of my half brothers from our board game. We watched, terrified, as law enforcement agents kicked down the front door of my father's place and stormed in.

When the law raids the home of a black man in America, it's not like you see on TV. It's mayhem and destruction. My brothers and I stood motionless as we watched the agents use large knives to slice open the couch cushions and pillows, and then pull out the white stuffing, haphazardly tossing it onto the carpet. Then they moved to the bedrooms and ripped into the mattresses.

I pleaded with an officer to let me go the bathroom. He made me pee in the bathtub—he thought I was trying to flush drugs. Nothing in that house was left untouched.

That included my father. They used brass knuckles to beat my dad, one of his friends, and even the dog. I was about eight years old when this happened, yet I can still hear the dog's yelps as the officers kicked him until he crawled into the corner, cowering and whining in pain and fear.

The house was destroyed. My brothers and I barely choked back our tears. Yet the one image that still haunts my memory today is the one of my father, hands cuffed behind his back, being walked out of the house. My brothers and I were sitting on the couch, shaking, when my father glanced over his shoulder at us. His eyes seared into mine. He never said anything. He never smiled. He just looked at me and my brothers and then turned back to the officer leading him to the police cruiser.

I still wonder what he was thinking in that moment. Was he embarrassed? Was he sad? Was he hurt that we had to see him cuffed like that? I don't know. But that look has never left me.

* * *

I remember another incident at my dad's house. He had a huge octagon table in his living room. In the middle of the table sat a deep dish, like a pounded-out metal bowl. It reminded me of a cauldron. One night, he hosted a party. People stumbled in and out, drinking and doing drugs in the living room, while I played with my Hot Wheels car. I drove the car around and around the octagon table.

I caught sight of a pile of white powder lying in the middle of the table. It looked like snow to me, so I drove the little metal car in and out, around in circles, and popped a few wheelies in the "snow." Suddenly, amid all the noise, my father stormed over and started yelling at me to get my Hot Wheels out of his coke.

Coke? What was that? I wondered. I know now, obviously.

I still wonder whether he was more upset because I was a kid playing with coke or because I was messing up his merchandise.

* * *

"JeVon, the only difference between the CEO of Budweiser and a drug dealer is one is selling legal drugs and the other isn't," my father would say to me. My father liked to remind me how society has decided what is and isn't legal, but underneath those declarations, it was all the same: one man trying to meet the needs of another man by selling him his product.

"In many ways, the drug dealer is smarter than the business-man," he would say to me, "because he has more hurdles to jump. He has to avoid the police. He has to avoid the IRS. He has to find ways to launder and stash his money. He has to find ways to continue to get his product into the country without getting caught and without going to prison. When a drug dealer gets caught, they go to prison. But the CEO of Budweiser, they're celebrated every time they make more money," he would say.

By no means was my father's chosen profession admirable or excusable. But it was these memories of my father—the moments when I saw how he navigated the streets, the tools he used to get what he wanted—that led me to an important realization. Depending on how you did things in the world and how you presented those things and yourself to society, it made the difference between whether you were successful and celebrated or admonished and jailed.

The CEO of Budweiser presents and packages an alcoholic beverage, which is legal. My father presented and packaged drugs, which were illegal. They were the same at their core, yet one was celebrated and the other hunted.

This idea stuck with me as I grew up. I understood that I could be a pimp and drug dealer living in the illegal world like my father, or I could be like the CEO of Budweiser, celebrated for selling something society deemed OK.

I decided I wanted to be legal. I mean, it only made sense to me. When was the last time you saw a retired pimp or drug dealer? You don't. There are no 401(k)s when you walk that road. If someone is making his money illegally, then he ends the game of life one of three ways: broke, in prison, or dead.

However, if you did things legally, if you looked and acted a certain way, you could be OK. What I did, how I presented it, and how I presented myself to society would make the difference.

I know this seems obvious to most people, but to those of us growing up poor and discarded from society, it's not.

* * *

I may not have any fond memories of my dad, but I can say that at least he was never physically or sexually abusive to me and my siblings.

But with the women he kept around, it was a different story.

I can't count the number of times I watched my dad beat a woman. It was such a regular occurrence that at some point, it no longer fazed me. It got to the point that when I was with my dad and he had a woman with us, I expected something to happen, like him slapping her silly, arguing loudly, jumping at her, or intimidating her into submission.

If it was just my dad and me or some half brothers (I didn't have many half sisters), everything was cool. But as soon as a woman showed up, I got on edge. It meant the peace was gone. Violence was coming.

As hard as it was to be around my father, some of the women he kept close were even worse. One in particular, Amber, my father's bottom bitch, was the most horrific of them all.

In the world of a pimp, the bottom bitch is the stable woman. Women cycle in and out, but the bottom, she sticks around no matter what. This one had been in my life since I was about four years old, and she was abusive in every way imaginable.

When I was about six or seven, she sexually assaulted me for the first time.

She undressed in front of me when my father left us alone to make a run. She demanded that I go down on her.

I put my face between her legs, and she started hitting me, yelling at me, "You ain't doing it right! DO IT RIGHT!"

I was petrified. And I had no idea what to do. She was so much bigger than me, and so mean, and kept hitting me, berating me.

This happened multiple times, but I didn't dare say anything to anyone.

Years later, I found out that she also molested one of my other brothers. He never said anything either.

* * *

I saw a lot of terrible things as a kid, and of all my father's girlfriends, Amber was the worst. But one of the worst moments for me was waking up at my father's and learning that my baby half sister had died in her sleep. I was told she died of sudden infant death syndrome.

It wasn't until my father's funeral, thirty years later, that I learned the truth: Amber suffocated her own baby.

Many people, like my mom and some of my half brothers and half sisters, knew the real story and confirmed it to me. I was the last one to learn that my half sister was smothered by that woman, her mother.

It's hard to say how my father took the death of my sister. He kept those feelings inside. He never spoke of her death.

Then, shortly after she died, he bought a new red Cadillac. I wouldn't be surprised if he bought that car with money he may have received after my sister's death.

Taking insurance policies out on your children is very unusual, but at the birth of each of his kids, he would take one out.

Yeah, this messed me up when I heard this, too. I have no idea why he would do something like that. But she was the only one of his kids who died young.

* * *

I never saw my father cry. He was a tough man. He grew up in the 1950s and dropped out of school at the age of fourteen.

He rarely talked about his past or family, but I remember one story he told me about his leather jacket. True to form for my father, he went out and hustled for money to buy himself a leather jacket. When he came home wearing his new coat, my grandfather asked him where he got the jacket. My dad told him that he went and bought it with his own money. My grandfather ripped it off him and threw it in the fireplace. "You need to help your mom out with bills and groceries instead of buying jackets!" he yelled at my dad.

That was the only story I heard about my grandfather.

I had my own leather jacket story with my dad, except mine was over a bag of candy. One weekend, when I was staying with my dad, I walked into the apartment with a bag of candy that I bought with some spare change. As soon as I walked in, my dad asked to see what I had. I tossed the bag to him and he pawed through the selection. He pulled out three of the pieces I wanted the most. I must have let out a heavy sigh or had a look on my face; whatever the case, my father didn't like my response.

He threw the bag at me. "Learn to share, JeVon," he scolded.

I snatched the bag and turned away, angry and hurt. *No one was sharing with me, so why should I share with them?* I thought. My father hurt my feelings. I was always the soft one out of all my brothers and sisters. I thank my mom for that; she protected and sheltered me from the harshness of street life, unlike my brothers and sisters who grew up tough. They were hardened by the reality of their everyday lives. Many of them had mothers who acted like my father.

Today, when I talk to my mom about some of my more horrific experiences at my father's, she's shocked. She thought she knew everything.

"Why didn't you ever tell me what was happening?" she says to me.

"Because I knew you wouldn't let me go back."

"Of *course* I would never have let you go back!"

"That's exactly why I didn't tell you."

Yes, my dad was a monster. Yes, he fathered twenty-three children—that he claimed. Yes, he was a pimp and a drug dealer. Yes, he beat women and did jail time.

But he was still my dad, and like any boy who longs for a father, I still wanted to spend time with mine. So I endured the traumatic experiences that came with being around him. They were better to me than losing him.

Unfortunately, I had no idea how bad things were going to get.

MY LIFE IN HOUSTON

When I was nine, my mom made a huge decision: she moved us from Dayton, Ohio, to Houston, Texas. At the time, I wasn't sure why. I knew my dad had moved to Houston months before. I assumed he was trying to avoid jail time. Later, I learned he had heard that the pimp game in Houston was alive and strong. He saw it as his own new frontier to make a killing. But my mom's decision never made sense to me. It wasn't like my parents ever lived together or were close.

It would take more than thirty-five years, but eventually, the truth came out.

"Do you know why I never said anything bad about your father?" my mom asked me one day.

"No, I never really questioned it. I've got my opinions. I know you have yours."

My mom looked at me for a long time, as though weighing whether she should say something or let it be. "Your dad kept me out of prison."

"What?" I couldn't believe what she had revealed to me. There I was in my forties, and this was the first time I had heard this. All that raced through my mind was, *What the hell?*

It turns out that my mom was wanted for welfare fraud. Back in the 1970s, my mom worked, but her job didn't pay enough to cover our living expenses. So she collected welfare, but even with those payments, we barely scraped by. However, you weren't allowed to work and collect welfare checks.

She faced prison time, but my dad, he knew everyone. The person who was going to prosecute my mom liked to use cocaine and have sex with prostitutes. Lo and behold, guess who was his drug dealer and pimp who set him up with women?

Yes, that's right; it was my dad.

All it took was drugs and women and my dad's connections to keep my mom out of jail. That was until the law enforcement official told my dad the only way for my mom to stay with me was if she left the state.

She didn't have a choice, and my dad couldn't do anything, so she packed us up and moved us to Houston.

When I learned what my father did for my mother, I was surprised. It helped me to better understand why my mom never said anything bad about him. Her memories of my father are distinct from mine. He was the guy who kept her out of jail and with her son. To me, he was the guy who left me standing at the window, falling asleep waiting for him. He was the guy who fathered twenty-three kids and never paid child support for any of us.

"He had some great qualities," my mom would say. I can't argue with her memory of my father. We had different experiences with him.

I just wish I knew what some of his great qualities were.

In Houston, my mom enrolled in college. Days were for classes and nights were spent working. She lived in what was called an adult apartment. Unfortunately, the building didn't allow children, so I had to live with my dad, his horrific girlfriend, Amber, and my two half sisters.

We arrived in the summer, and at first, we lived at a weekly rate motel. The only good things about that weekly motel were I learned to swim in the motel's pool and I liked the bowling alley across the street. It had video games.

My dad and his girlfriend used the motel for their normal business operations. I remember one sweltering summer day, when, as a nine-year-old boy, I was left to watch my six-month-old baby sister. My dad was gone. I had no idea where he was, and Amber was out trying to find the next trick to turn. For those who aren't familiar with what a trick means, a trick is a guy who's paying for sex.

I can still hear my sister, wearing nothing but a diaper, crying, her screams echoing in the room as I tried holding her, rocking her, walking her—anything I could think of to get her to calm down. "What do you need?" I pleaded with her, knowing that she couldn't answer me. *Did she need her diaper changed?* I wondered. I didn't even know

how to change a diaper. *Was she hungry?* I thought. I had
no idea how to fix a bottle.

I was terrified and without anyone to turn to. It was the
first time I was without the protection of my mother. At
least when I was in Dayton and my dad picked me up for
a couple of nights, I knew I would always return to my
mom. Not this time, though. This time I was alone, and
I had no idea how to make my baby sister stop crying. I
tried everything I could think of to make her stop crying,
but nothing worked.

Frustrated, scared, and just wanting her to stop, I roughly
tossed her onto the couch.

My body froze the moment she left my arms. Horrified at
what I'd done, I raced to her and scooped her into my arms.
I held her tightly to my chest whispering, "I'm sorry. I'm so
sorry," over and over again, tears streaming from my eyes.

I think about this moment a lot. To be honest, it haunts
me. I feel like this is the worst thing I've ever done. What
kind of monster throws a six-month-old child?

I did.

As I was trying to comfort my little sister and get her to stop crying, Amber showed up with a trick. She needed the room to work, so she told me to take my sister outside. There I stood with my sister in my arms. She was still wearing only her diaper and she was still crying.

I tried walking her up and down the cement walkway in front of the motel rooms. I tried bouncing her and whispering softly to her as I walked into the parking lot. Nothing worked.

It was only 10:30 a.m., not even time for lunch, yet the Houston sun beat down on us. The muggy, humid air wrapped around our skin. I can still feel my sister's small body grow sweaty and damp in my arms.

This was the first time I'd ever been away from my mom. I was nine years old, with a six-month-old child in my arms, and I was scared. I didn't know what to do.

Making sales calls, scaling a business, studying balance sheets and income statements, losing weight, figuring out how to make money in the stock market—all of that is so easy to me. Nothing in my adult life compares to what I felt that day in Houston. The stresses that I face now aren't even stresses to me. They're easy.

Being a nine-year-old kid, forced to take care of a six-month-old baby, all alone—now *that's hard.*

As fall approached and the school year was about to begin, my dad got a real job in a high-end department store that paid him wages. He moved us from the weekly motel into public housing, and for the first time in my life, I had a sense of normalcy. Every day, he got up and went to work regular hours like other fathers. And sometimes, on the weekends, he took me to ride go-karts.

It was the calmest my life had ever been.

* * *

While we lived in public housing, I had the chance to join the Boy Scouts, which I called the Ghetto Scouts. There was a Boy Scout jamboree that we desperately wanted to attend. But those events cost money—money most of us didn't have. To raise money for the trip, we decided to hold a car wash at a nearby church. Our troop was determined to go to the jamboree.

Our idea worked! People lined up with their cars; we soaked the dusty vehicles with water and soap, rinsed the suds off, and people handed us money for a job well done. We worked hard, laughed, and delighted in collecting enough money to pay for a trip to the jamboree.

We were excited and proud of our efforts, but then the money was stolen.

I mean, of course it was, right?

In one swipe, all our hard work and the money we earned was gone, and with it our dreams of the jamboree. That was until our story made it on the nightly news, and by the grace of a kind citizen who donated the money we needed, our troop made it to the jamboree.

A sad moment was transformed into an exciting one—until the day of the jamboree, when we found out we weren't like the other troops.

Each Boy Scout troop could take part in different contests. One contest was on the appearance of your uniform. As a bunch of poor kids who lived in public housing, no one had a complete outfit. One boy had the scarf, another the socks, and one person had the hat. Maybe if we had taken a piece of clothing from each of us we'd be able to assemble a complete uniform.

When the jamboree officials saw us, they pulled us off to the side. They wouldn't let us take part. Tears spilled from our eyes, and we wiped our cheeks on the sleeves of our ratty shirts. We got left out. We were the poor troop, the troop that lived in public housing and couldn't afford the right uniforms.

This had a profound effect on me. Like I said, growing up

poor forces you to understand hard realities. Money is not everything, but in many cases, not having it means you get nothing.

*   *   *

I've lived in a lot of places over the years, and one thing is always the same: broke is broke and poor is poor wherever you live. It may not have been inner-city Dayton, but I was still living in poverty when I was in Houston. The same was true of everyone around me. The only "newness" in my immediate surroundings was the introduction of a new ethnicity. Suddenly, I was living shoulder to shoulder with Mexicans. In Dayton, as I've said before, it was only black or white. In Houston, there was a third option.

I had never seen brown people, and many times in Houston, because of my mixed race, people confused me for Mexican. For the first time in my nine years of life, I felt more accepted for the color of my skin. No one discriminated against me over my race like they did in Dayton.

The city itself was enormous, and there was wealth like I'd never witnessed in Houston.

"Take me for a ride, Dad," I'd beg. "Take me to see those giant houses!"

Dad would drive me downtown, and I'd look out the backseat window at the skyscrapers, the fancy cars, and blocks of downtown corridor. To this day, I still have a fetish over these things; I love to look at them. I'd stare at the streets mobbed with people and watch, mesmerized by the hustle and bustle of commercial activity, of money being exchanged. Businesses thrived. All of this activity, this wealth, was new to me. Nothing and no one thrived in Dayton. Wealth and Dayton did not belong in the same sentence.

We'd go to the rich neighborhoods like River Oaks, where the ten-thousand-square-foot, $10 million homes were. As we drove by, I'd stare at them in awe. I'd never seen such large homes. I couldn't believe they were real and that people lived in them.

And I can clearly remember thinking to myself, *I want one of those for myself.*

It was in Houston when a desire for the nice home, the luxury cars, and the life of celebration and comfort gripped me.

I saw how other people lived in those big homes and fancy cars. Then I saw how I lived in poverty and one misstep away from a life of crime, punishment, and loss. Seeing that there was another way to live sparked something in me. It was the beginning of a tiny flame—one that would turn into a wildfire that would fuel me.

It was a desire to win the game.

* * *

Living in Houston with my father was the most time I'd ever spent with the man. While I was happy to have him in my life more, it was hard, too, because I rarely saw my mom. Between school and work, she didn't have a lot of time. And when she did have time, it was hard for her to come and get me. She didn't have a license and didn't know how to drive. (She didn't start driving until she was thirty-five.)

When we spent time together, one of the things we did was play the board game Monopoly. It was one of the few games I owned, along with Candy Land.

My mom actually taught me how to play the board game around the age of five, and very quickly, I realized the secret to winning: be the one to control the money. Most people clambered to buy the big properties like Boardwalk and Park Place. I wasn't everyone. I wanted the railroads. If I owned all the railroads, then every time someone landed on one, they had to give me $200. And everyone lands on the railroads the entire game. I wanted the continuous stream of money rather than the big one- or two-time prizes. (That attitude toward the game would become my investing philosophy later in life, too.)

When I look at life, it reminds me of Monopoly. There are rules to how the game is played, just like there are rules to how you win in society. These rules cover things like dressing a certain way, speaking a certain way, and displaying a certain work ethic. We don't get to write the rules of society, but we can learn the rules and adapt our skills to them, and it is possible for us to beat society at its own game.

There's no fairness in either game. People aren't given breaks or money because they deserve them, in Monopoly or in life. The world is cruel and it's harsh. But the rules are the same for everyone and can be learned and used.

When I played Monopoly with other people, and they realized the game wasn't going their way, they'd want to quit. I never let them. The way I see it, if there's no quitting in life, then there's no letting someone win. Even today, I don't let people win games. As my children grow up, I won't let them win games either because that isn't how the world works.

I grew up believing that if I wanted to win at the game of life, if I wanted to have a fancy home and nice car like the ones I saw in Houston, then I had to control the money, just like I did in Monopoly. It's the person who controls the money who wins the game. And the only person I could count on to win the game was me. No one was coming to save me; no one was going to let me win.

This perspective drove me as an adult, but before I reached those years, I had to learn what landing on the "Go to Jail" space meant.

THREE

Incarceration

———

I SPENT LESS THAN A YEAR IN HOUSTON, AND BY THE age of ten, I was back in Dayton, Ohio. The reason? Dad tried to live a humble man's life; he tried to leave the drug-dealing and pimp-hustler ways behind him.

But he failed.

A normal life could not coexist with my father. He may have had a humble job, but my father was far from a humble man. He couldn't swallow his pride, and he couldn't adjust to the cut in income that came from leaving his pimp and drug dealer lifestyle. He couldn't hack it in Houston, so he left and returned to the life that he knew in Dayton.

He just didn't tell any of us about his plans.

I came home from school one day, and he was gone, leaving me behind with Amber and my two half sisters.

This wasn't Dad's first or only failed attempt at making a legitimate living. In Dayton, he tried his hand at owning a nightclub, and he managed a few of the 1970s bands out of the area, like the Ohio Players and Slave. These bands had some big hits in the late 1970s and early 1980s, and I remember being at parties with my dad and the groups. Of course, there was coke and prostitutes at these gatherings, supplied by my father. My dad even tried his hand at owning a recording studio; he was the first person in Dayton to do this.

One of my half brothers said it best, "The problem with Dad was he lacked execution." My dad was a dreamer. He had great ideas, and for moments, he had direction. However, he couldn't seem to make the jump from the three-dollar-hustler-pimp to legitimacy.

The business world is filled with dreamers like my father. Dreams and visions are good things to have, but you need the discipline to execute. Execution is what turns your dreams into reality.

My dad's attempt at a legitimate job in Houston lasted from roughly July to March. I don't know why, but I finished the fifth grade in Houston, even after my dad abandoned us. Then one day, my dad's girlfriend decided she'd had enough of the Lone Star state. She wanted to return to Dayton and I had to go with her. Mom was still living in the adult apartment that didn't allow children, working, and going to school. She didn't have the means to support the two of us, so staying in Houston wasn't an option for me.

As we packed the U-Haul, I asked to say good-bye to my mom, but I was told no, that my mom was too busy. I never got to say good-bye to my mom. I never got to give her one last hug. I never got to hear her say, "I love you, JeVon," one last time.

Later, I learned how my mom found out that I'd moved. It breaks my heart knowing this, but as the story goes, she tried unsuccessfully for more than a week to reach me. Finally, between work and school, she was able to go to the apartment we lived in. Sadly, she discovered it was empty.

I was gone.

No one had bothered to tell her we were moving back to Dayton. We left her, just like my father had left us. Neither my mom nor I knew that it would be two long years before we were briefly reunited.

I missed my mom terribly, and it upset me that I didn't get

to say good-bye. Yet I was looking forward to spending more time with my dad. I thought he'd be happier in his life. I thought we'd be a family.

But I was very, very wrong.

My return to Dayton was a turning point in my life. The first nine years of my life (until I moved to Houston) were tough. My mom and I struggled, never having quite enough money, but they weren't terrible. My mom protected me as best she could from the harsh world surrounding us. I was loved. I was cherished. I was safe.

But going back to Dayton without my mom changed everything for the worse. The next three and a half years of my life would be my own private hell, a horror movie that I had to live through day after day. Being sexually molested was nothing compared to what I was about to go through.

FOUR

Disaster in Ohio

———

FROM THE AGES OF TEN TO THIRTEEN, I LIVED OFF AND ON with my father or one of his girlfriends. When I look back on this time, it wasn't that I suffered direct abuse by my father's hands. His sin was neglect.

He wasn't around to offer me any guidance or protection from the horrors of his life or the troubled women around him. Instead, I had to deal with life myself. Alone.

One of the worst experiences came when I was thirteen years old. It was January 2, and my father said he was going to England for two weeks. I didn't see him again until December 23, almost a year later. That was the longest two-week vacation in the history of mankind.

We were living with the same girlfriend, Amber, but now she and my father had three kids: my two half sisters, who were three and four, and my half brother, who was two. I remember watching him drive away and feeling an aching sense of loneliness. My mom was still in Texas and Amber was a nightmare. My older half brother, Aaron, happened to be with us, too. In a way, he was like a protector for me. But two weeks into my father's English excursion, Aaron's mom came and took him away.

Again, I watched him, like I had watched my father, drive away. I blinked back tears as I thought about how my mom couldn't come and pick me up like Aaron's mother.

God, I missed Aaron when he left. Where he had been the buffer between me and Amber, now it was just me and her and my little sisters and brother. I was truly alone.

About a month and a half after my father left, Amber said she was going to the store to buy a pack of cigarettes.

She left in the afternoon, but when the evening came, she was still gone. I put my sisters and brother to bed on the living room floor, hoping Amber would be back soon. But the next morning came and still no sign of her. Then two days passed, then three. By day five, I realized she wasn't coming back. I was supposed to be in school, but I couldn't leave my sisters and brother alone.

We were about to run out of food, and it was up to me to take care of everyone. I told my four-year-old sister to sit down and make sure the other two sat still. "You guys watch television until I get back, OK?" I told them. Everyone looked at me and nodded. "I'm going to the store to get us some food."

Leaving my brother and sisters locked in the house, I trudged in the snow to the corner store. I slipped through the doors and walked down the empty aisles. When no one was looking, I sneaked food into my pockets and bag and rushed outside.

By day seven, we were still alone, but now we were without diapers for my two-year-old brother, Mario. Food was easy to sneak into my pockets, but diapers? There was no way I could steal those without getting caught, so I did the only thing I could think of.

I potty trained Mario.

I held him down on the toilet, and every time he tried to get up, I forced him back down. Tears streamed down his face and mine as I apologized over and over to him for what

I was doing. "Hey, I'm sorry, man," I said to him. "I don't know what else to do. You got to go potty."

Having my own children now and knowing what it's like for a two-year-old, well, it rips me apart what I had to do with Mario. But I was thirteen and had no idea what else to do and no one to call to help us. Hell, we didn't have a phone.

Everyone and everything was on my shoulders.

Nine days into our ordeal, I realized it was my middle sister's birthday. So I returned to the grocery store and stole a package of Oreo cookies and candles. Back at the house, I twisted off the tops of the cookies and stuck three candles in the white cream filling. Everyone gathered around and we sang "Happy Birthday."

My sister clapped her hands and giggled when she saw her "cake." She pretended to blow out the candles while I actually blew them out. Then we spent the rest of the day munching on the crumbling cookies.

When I told this story to a friend, he wanted to know how I was this resourceful at the age of thirteen. All credit goes to my mom because she was always creative. No matter how much we struggled, it was important to my mom that I had moments of joy, especially around holidays and my birthday. When I realized it was my sister's birthday, it was important to me that she had a moment of joy, too. I tried to think, *What would Mom do if this was my birthday?*

Even today, I'm driven by this need for the people in my life, whether it's my family and friends, my employees, or my customers, to have incredible experiences. As a CEO, I'm good with budgets, line items, and numbers. But running a business is more than numbers. I'm constantly looking at how we can improve the human experience or our services. That's one of the secrets to success, no matter what position you hold in a company.

I see business being about the relationship you have with people. When you care about the experience of the people you're working with, and you care about the people you're serving, then results are easy.

* * *

I cared for my brother and sisters for three weeks. Not once did I go to school, and I swear the owners of the corner grocery store knew I was stealing food, but they never said anything.

When the girlfriend, Amber, showed up, my brothers and sisters ran into her arms. I stood back, my arms crossed and a scowl on my face. I let the kids have their moment and when they settled down, I had mine.

"Where the *fuck* have you been?" I yelled. I was furious at her for leaving us.

Amber was silent as she stalked toward me. Once she got within striking distance, she leveled me with a punch so hard that it knocked me to the ground and blood trickled from my ear. Once I was on the floor, she kicked me in the ribs and the stomach, then she punched me in the face and arms. Whatever body part she could beat, she unleashed her fury on me.

Eventually, she settled down and left me in a heap on the floor. I crawled to my feet, then ran up the stairs to my bedroom as fast as my bruised body could move.

I couldn't take it anymore. I couldn't stay with her. I crawled out my bedroom window, slid down the drainage pipe, and ran away.

I had nowhere to go, so I went to my uncle Bobby's. My uncle Bobby was the opposite of my dad. He was a stern Christian type of man. I begged him to let me live with him, but he had three kids of his own and a grandson he was caring for. He didn't have the space or money to take me in, too, so he brought me back to my father's. Amber didn't take kindly to my running away and proceeded to beat me again for my disrespect.

I think the second beating I caught may have been worse than the first one, if that's possible.

After that incident, another uncle came and took me from Amber's care. He brought me to a different girlfriend of my father's. She lived in the suburbs and had two older boys. I showed up with my mother's old, tattered, teal suitcase, the one she had left the orphanage with. I had no clue what was happening or where I was. I didn't know this woman or her sons. It was mass confusion, but they were nice. The boys treated me like a little brother. It felt kind of cool. I had my own room, the woman bought me new clothes, I went to school each day, and we ate dinner together—all of us, every night. I had a normal routine again, and I loved it.

That first week was great until the weekend arrived and the boys' father came to pick them up. I was left with the girlfriend, and this is when I discovered she was an alcoholic. As soon as her sons left, she started drinking, and when she drank, she beat me.

Once, she beat me so badly that I broke. I was tired of being beaten by her, so I fought back. It's not hard to beat up a drunk old woman, and I kicked her ass. Bad.

I think I snapped because I felt weak. For five days, I thought

I'd made it out. I thought the bad times were behind me, all the bullshit was past, and I was safe now.

But all of that was fake. The suburbs, the food, the niceness—it was all fake. I was still getting my ass beat; I was just getting my ass beat in a really nice house with a full belly.

Unfortunately, she called the police on me, and I was sent to juvenile detention. It was the first of what would be three stays.

Later on, in juvie, I wondered to myself if I'd made the right decision. Maybe the beatings were worth it if it kept me in a house like that and out of juvenile detention.

DOING TIME IN JUVIE

I did three stints in juvenile detention while my father was in England for a year. The first time wasn't bad, but I remember it being chaotic. Most boys were as angry and frustrated as I was. I wasn't there long before my Aunt Jean, my father's sister, came to pick me up with my mom's raggedy suitcase filled with my clothes. Instead of bringing me to one of my dad's girlfriends' homes, she tried to keep me with relatives and dropped me off at her sister, my Aunt Cindy's, place.

A few days into my stay at Aunt Cindy's, I overheard Aunt Cindy talking to her husband, Uncle Walter. They weren't arguing, just discussing how they couldn't afford to feed me.

My chest felt heavy when I heard this. I knew I couldn't stay with them, and I didn't want to go back to one of the girlfriends' homes. So I did the only thing I could think of: I threw my few belongings into my mom's old tattered suitcase and quietly slipped into the night without telling anyone.

I had no idea where to go, just that I needed some type of shelter. I decided to make my home at a bus stop, at least some were encased with Plexiglas windows. The one I chose wasn't completely enclosed, but there was enough covering that it kept some of the wind and chill of the night off me. I found a small spot in the corner to curl up. There I laid on the cold concrete, clutching my mother's suitcase to my chest, and I wept.

God, I missed my mother. I was scared and alone. I wanted her to come and protect me, but I had no way to reach her. I didn't have her number or her address. I didn't even know if she knew where I was or what had been happening in my life. I closed my eyes, trying to shut out the pain of my life, and hugged the suitcase tighter to my chest, imagining it was my mom wrapping her arms around me in a giant hug.

For four nights, this is how I fell asleep at the bus stop—crying and pretending that my mom was beside me.

During the day, I went to school. It was a safe haven. I had some friends, so I was able to ask for their leftovers at lunch, and sometimes I got a little girl to buy me lunch. I'd stay as long as I could at school before they kicked me out. I'd shower in the locker room and put on fresh clothes that I pulled from my suitcase. I had my clothes neatly divided in piles between clean and dirty. Because I was living on the streets, I had no place to stash my suitcase, which meant I had to carry it with me to school. It was too big to fit inside my locker, so I brought it with me from class to class.

Thirteen-year-old kids in middle school can be cruel. They're harsh in the worst ways. When kids caught me lugging my tattered suitcase in the hallways, they poked fun at me. Of course, I was embarrassed over my situation. I missed my mom, and I didn't want to be the kid without a place to call home. I didn't want to be the kid who carried his dirty and clean clothes to school.

I remember one boy was relentless in his teasing. I tried to ignore him, but one day, I couldn't take it anymore. I snapped and lashed out at him. I unleashed all the rage I was carrying inside of me onto him, punching him again and again, completely out of control. I pummeled him until people dragged me off the boy's listless body.

The beating I had given to him was so severe that I put him in a coma.

The police came and carted me off to juvenile detention (my second stint), where I sat alone for two months without anyone knowing where I was. Because I'd lived on the streets before my arrest, my family, like Aunt Jean, lost track of me. My dad was still in England and my mom was in Texas. Neither of them knew I was behind bars, and I had no way of contacting them either.

I hurt. If my mom had known I was in juvie, she would have come for me. She would have found a way to rescue me from that cell.

This was the hardest stint I endured in juvenile detention. To a thirteen-year-old kid, two months feels like twenty years. Every night, I laid on my small cot with a scratchy blanket tucked under my chin, praying that when I woke up, I'd be back in my mom's tiny apartment in Dayton.

I cried. I wanted to go back to the days when it was just me and Mom trying our best to get by together.

During those two months, every night I wished that Mom and I were standing at the bus stop again, in the rain or snow, with bread bags on our feet. I wished we were lugging black Hefty lawn bags filled with dirty clothes to the laundromat. I wished that we were eating a pack of lima beans for dinner. I made so many wishes those nights. But wishing did nothing for me. I woke up in the same place. This is when I eliminated the words *hope* and *wish* from my vocabulary. I was like the ghetto Yoda—there was only "do" and "do not" and that's it.

My childhood, this time especially, taught me that wishing and hoping were useless. Wishing never gave me a free lunch ticket when I went through the line without one. Hoping never gave me a chocolate milk when Mom couldn't scrounge up the extra ten cents. Wishing never made the bus come faster, and hoping never gave us a car. Wishing never put food on the dinner table, and hoping never gave my mom change for the bus fare so we didn't have to walk. Wishing didn't make my mom show up to save me from juvie, and hoping didn't make my living nightmare go away.

No, wishing and hoping had no meaning in my life, and they didn't help me to triumph over my challenges.

If you want something in this world, be it professionally or personally, then you have to go out and get it. You have to do something. You have to drive forward, push through, and believe that you will get what you want. You have to keep going no matter what, never stopping until you succeed.

That's a mindset I developed over time, but at that particular moment in juvie, I felt trapped. I felt like there was no light at the end of the tunnel for me.

The only saving grace, if you can call it that, was my reputation with the other kids. Word had spread that I was in juvenile detention because I put a kid in a coma. That meant no one fucked with me. It also meant that I was truly alone.

In a strange way, I have my mother to thank for getting me out, even if she had no idea I was locked away. My mom chose the name JeVon because it was the name of a French character in a book she had once read. By no means was this a popular name, especially in the seventies or early eighties in Dayton. Around the eight-week mark of my stay, a woman who worked in corrections recognized my name. "Do you have an Aunt Jean?" she asked.

"Yeah, that's my aunt."

The next day, Aunt Jean appeared. The woman had called my aunt and told her where I was. She explained to Aunt

Jean that no one had been to visit or to get me in two months. Without any questions, without expecting anything in return, Aunt Jean picked me up.

* * *

It's fitting that Aunt Jean was the one to pick me up from juvie. During the year my father was out of the country, it was always Aunt Jean who showed up when I needed help. She was in my life for most of the five years I spent back in Dayton with my dad (I lived there from the ages of ten to fifteen), but that year he was gone was the year I was in and out of juvenile detention. I think this was when she realized I was in a bad situation and that I had no one. It was always Aunt Jean who picked me up when I was in juvie; it was always Aunt Jean who tried hard to find me a stable home with relatives or at one of my dad's girlfriends' homes.

When I stayed with my dad's girlfriends, many nights I didn't want to go back. I didn't want a beating from them or to take any more of their abuse. I would stay out on the streets as long as I could, until I realized if I didn't go back then I had no place to go for the night. Then I'd think of Aunt Jean.

I'd call Aunt Jean at ten-thirty or eleven at night, and without question or hesitation, she'd crawl out of bed, get dressed, pick me up, and then get me something to eat, usually a burger, soda, and fries from a drive-through. It didn't matter where I was. I could be on the other side of town or at a middle school dance, and Aunt Jean would come for me. A lot of times she'd bring me home with her. She even bought me school clothes when I needed them, and she'd slip a few dollars into my pocket when she saw me. I remember her hugs—she always gave me a hug—and for that brief moment, I felt a little bit of love. It was a reminder of my mom, a reminder of what it's like to have someone care about you and for your well-being.

I was told she couldn't have children of her own, and I always believed that's why she was there for me whenever I needed someone. Later in life, I learned she was that person for many of my twenty-three half brothers and half sisters, too. Her generosity and kindness toward all of us blows my mind.

If you tried to thank her for helping you, she would get mad. "You don't thank me for feeding you," she'd order. "You're my family. If you need a meal, I'm going to make sure you eat."

Aunt Jean never took us in. She was amazing to us, bought us food and clothes, but she never took any of us in, ever. I'm not sure why. Maybe it was because she couldn't have kids herself and it was too painful for her, or maybe it was because her husband, Uncle Mose, didn't like kids. Or maybe there were just too many of us to take care of.

Whatever the case, it doesn't matter. I'm still thankful that Aunt Jean was there for me. I'm still grateful for her being in my life, because who knows where I would be today if she hadn't been there for me during that year of hell.

Even though I knew Aunt Jean would be there for me whenever I needed her, I still felt guilty for calling her.

I wondered how many times she was going to pick me up from juvie or late at night. Even at the young age of thirteen, I was hyperaware that I didn't want to abuse Aunt Jean's generosity.

The five years I lived in Dayton with my father, I didn't have a lot of people I could count on. My father wasn't someone who was capable of guiding, caring, and parenting me. But Aunt Jean was someone I could always count on to show up. And back then, that was huge for me.

Eventually, I lost touch with Aunt Jean. It wasn't until I was in my early thirties when I found myself thinking about her a lot. I found her number and called the house. My Uncle Mose answered.

"May I speak with Aunt Jean?"

"Who's this?"

"This is JeVon. Is this Uncle Mose?"

"Yeah. Hey, how you doing, son?"

I told him about my life, my success in business, the home
I owned, and other small details about my life. He seemed
happy and maybe a bit proud, too, of where I was in life.
We were running out of things to say, so I asked again to
speak with Aunt Jean.

There was a heavy sigh on the other end of the line. "Son,
I'm sorry. No one told you?"

"Told me what?"

"Your Aunt Jean died over a year ago."

Man, that crushed me. Even today, I'm still sad that I never got
a chance to say "thank you" to her for all that she did for me.

Even though she isn't here to read this, I still need to say
it. Thank you, Aunt Jean. You meant more to me than you
probably know.

LIVING WITHOUT MOM

Between the ages of ten and fifteen, I saw my mom once, right before my father left on his trip to England. I was twelve at the time. Some of my dad's friends planned a trip to Houston, so he asked them if I could hitch a ride. They let me, but I was the outcast in the car. They were all family, and they didn't take kindly to a strange boy tagging along.

I hardly remember the car ride, but I do remember they were mean to me. When we arrived in Houston, all I cared about was seeing my mom. "Hey, are we going to the meeting place, so I can see my mom?" I asked.

"We'll go when we go, kid."

After running their errands and who knows what else this crew needed doing, they brought me to the drop-off stop to meet my mom. We pulled up. My stomach clenched and my body tingled when I saw her get out of the car. I flung open the car door and sprinted to her as she raced toward me. As soon as I was close enough, I launched myself into her arms. Her arms encircled me, gripping me so tightly to her that I could barely breathe. I didn't care. There, in the parking lot, I wept into her shoulder, clutching the back of her shirt in my fists. I never wanted to let her go.

I cried for the years we were apart. I cried for how warm

it felt to be back in the arms of my protector, my shelter, and with the person who loved and cared for me the most. I cried because I was home; Mom was home.

Both of us stood weeping and clinging to each other, like some cliché scene from a Hollywood movie. I can only imagine what we must have looked like to people on the sidewalk. Eventually, we untangled our arms from each other and got into her car.

This was the first time I'd EVER seen my mom drive. All I had ever known was her and I on the bus or walking. She gripped the wheel tightly with both hands, trying to focus on the traffic and talk to me at the same time. I can't remember what we talked about, but I do remember I couldn't take my eyes off her. I hadn't seen her in two years!

And while I had missed her terribly, I wasn't prepared for how deep that pain ran. It wasn't until we sat in her car that I realized just how lost and alone I had felt.

We went to a McDonald's drive-through for dinner, which may not seem like such a big deal, but it was. The last time we were together, Mom could barely scrape together ten cents to buy me a chocolate milk. Now, she was driving and buying me hamburgers, fries, and sodas. We took our food back to her tiny apartment where we spent the night talking and just being together.

It was one of the best nights ever, but it hurt, too. It hurt because as soon as I walked into her place, I could see how hard she was still struggling to get by. I desperately wanted to ask her if I could stay with her forever. But when I saw how sparsely furnished the apartment was, when I saw how little food she had in the fridge, I couldn't bring myself to ask that of her. It was hard enough for her to get by on her own, so how could I ask her to care for me, too?

I wanted to be back with my mom, to be safe and protected, but I couldn't ask. I knew she would take me in, but I couldn't do that to her.

I didn't tell her about the abuse and neglect I was enduring. I kept quiet because I wanted to protect her. I knew she couldn't afford to take care of me, and if I told her what was happening in Dayton, she'd worry about my safety. I couldn't put her through that; she didn't deserve to have more stress added to her life.

When she asked me how I was doing, I smiled and said what I believed she needed and wanted to hear. "Everything's great, Mom. Yeah, I'm fine," I told her. Of course, I was far from fine, and it was a bald-faced lie. The last thing I wanted was to go back to Dayton, but I didn't see another path for my life.

We had one night together in Houston, and then I had to return to Dayton. Leaving my mom was the most emotional moment of my life. When I returned to Dayton, I was a beast; I was mad and angry at the world. If someone had given me a gas can and matches, I would have lit the world on fire. I was an emotional wreck.

* * *

My third trip to juvenile detention, for stealing food, was my last. I give credit to one of the correctional officers for steering me toward the straight and narrow.

As I gathered my things to leave juvie, a correctional officer came up to me and said, "Look here, son. You could be somebody. Don't come back here."

I nodded my head, not really listening to him, and that's when he looked sharply at me. "Let me tell you this. There are a lot of boys in here headed to *man prison*. If you come back here again, you're going to end up in *man prison*, too. Is that what you want? To go to *man prison*? You know what that place is like?"

The officer's words struck fear in me. "Man prison" sounded

bad, and to this day, I still shiver when I say that phrase. At that age, I didn't know what "man prison" was, but I knew I didn't want to find out. I sure as hell knew I didn't want to go. Even as an adult, I still don't want to know.

Like always, my Aunt Jean was the one to pick me up from juvie. This time, she was bringing me to my Uncle Bobby, who'd agreed to take me in. As I sat in Aunt Jean's car with my mother's old suitcase on my lap, the officer's words to me replayed over and over. All I could think was, *I don't want to go to man prison. I don't want to go to man prison,* and that was it for me. Game over. I was done screwing up and landing in juvenile detention.

Once I make my mind up, once I say I'm going to do something, I do it. It was time to find another way to get where I wanted to go.

THINGS CAN ALWAYS GET WORSE...OR BETTER

Growing up, Mom liked to remind me that people had it worse than us. She was right, and I've used that line to remind me to appreciate everything and everyone that I have in my life, in every moment. Each night, when I stand in front of my home, I'm reminded of where I've come from. The five years between the ages of ten and fifteen, when I lived off and on with my father, are the ones that really stand out. I'm reminded of what I've accomplished and the road I took to get to where I am today. Gratitude is important, and my mom's thinking has helped to ground me as I've risen out of poverty, overcome abuse and neglect, and triumphed over racism.

But even as a young boy, when I heard my mom's words, I also thought, *Well, there are people better off than us, too. Why can't we be like them?*

I had seen them in Houston. I saw their houses. I saw their lives. They were what I wanted. There was a way out of the hood because I saw other people living a different life, and I wanted it, too. I wanted to get there, to get where those people were.

Instead of focusing on the ones worse off than me, I decided to focus on those better off than me. I figured that if I'm going to think, then I'm going to think big. It takes the same amount of energy to think small as it does to think big, to think about what could be, and to think about what I could make happen.

I chose to focus on the people who had more than us, who were better off than us, and who achieved more than us because I *believed* that I, too, could get there.

Even during these horrific years in Dayton, I believed things could get better for me. I wasn't sure how or when, but I knew my life could be better than what I was experiencing. This belief carried with me throughout my teenage years, into adulthood, and it's a mentality I still have today.

I've never told myself that I can't do something. If I wanted it, I did it. If I had to learn how to do it, I learned how to do it.

The truth is, things can always get worse in life, but the other side is that things can also *always* get better.

The year my father lived in England and I was left to fend for myself was maybe the most awful year of my life. But the moment Aunt Jean picked me up from my third stint in juvenile detention and brought me to live with my Uncle Bobby was the moment my life took a turn. Things got better.

FIVE

Uncle Bobby

———

"WE'RE LEAVING AT TEN O'CLOCK SATURDAY MORNING,"
Uncle Bobby said to me, my three cousins, and aunt during
dinner on Friday night. I'd been living with Uncle Bobby for
three months, and he was taking us on a church vacation
to West Virginia. Uncle Bobby was a strict disciplinarian,
whereas my aunt was the nice, easygoing pushover. They
balanced each other that way.

Saturday morning came, and my aunt said she needed to
go to the grocery store to buy cashews and peanuts for my
uncle. "Look, I'm leaving at ten o'clock," Uncle Bobby said
matter-of-factly. Everyone, including my uncle, knew she
had forgotten something—she wasn't going for just Uncle
Bobby's snacks.

My cousins, who always sided with my easygoing, nice aunt, went with her. I stayed behind with Uncle Bobby to finish packing the van.

I also stayed with Uncle Bobby because it didn't take me long to realize he was the one who had all the money. As I had learned watching my father and his hustler ways, and from playing Monopoly: the one who controls the money controls life.

Uncle Bobby and I packed the van. As ten o'clock got closer, I ran to the bottom of the driveway and looked down the street. No sign of my aunt and cousins. *Man, where are they?* I thought nervously.

"Uncle Bobby, I'm going to run upstairs and get my football."

"Son, I know what you're doing." He fixed me with a level gaze. "I'm leaving at ten o'clock."

I ran upstairs, grabbed my football, and raced back to the driveway. We stood by the van for a few minutes. Uncle Bobby glanced at his wristwatch, nodded his head once, then slid the van door shut.

"OK, JeVon, get in."

My eyes widened in surprise, but I did as I was told. You always did what Uncle Bobby said.

This was back in the early 1980s, before people had cell phones or pagers. We had no way of getting in touch with my aunt. As I climbed into the passenger seat, I expected my aunt to appear and half-expected we were going to wait in the van for them.

What I didn't expect was for Uncle Bobby to start the engine and to drive off—without the rest of his family.

The ride to West Virginia was a mixture of astonishment over what Uncle Bobby did and excitement and curiosity over this thing called a vacation. I had no idea what you did on a vacation. Along the way, we stopped at gas stations and Uncle Bobby bought me snacks, which was the most awesome thing ever.

It took us six or seven hours to get to the hotel, and when we did, we checked into our room, then ran errands. We returned with bags of food and were met by quite a surprise: my aunt and cousins.

As soon as my aunt saw Uncle Bobby, she laid into him. There was my nice, easygoing aunt yelling at my uncle. I'd never heard her yell!

The entire time he stood there, looking her straight in the eyes and taking her tirade. After about five minutes, she calmed down. He took the opening. "Are you finished?" he asked.

"Yes," she snapped.

He flipped his wrist around and looked down at the watch. Then he turned his gaze—it was almost emotionless—to her. "I said ten o'clock," he said simply, and then he turned his back on her and walked away.

I was transfixed at the scene in front of me, and if I had any doubt before about my uncle's strict discipline and utter commitment to keeping his word, it was erased in that moment. Whoa, this man is so structured and disciplined that he left his family behind on a vacation.

This story has stayed with me, and I joke with my wife all the time when we're getting ready to go out to dinner or to an event. I tell her, "Don't make me go Uncle Bobby in here."

This one moment had such an impact on me that UBT became legendary in one company that I led. UBT stands for Uncle Bobby Time, and it meant that if we had a conference call or a meeting, it was on UBT. If you weren't in the room by the time the meeting was scheduled to start, we started without you. Punctuality is key to me and one of the many lessons I took with me into the business world.

Punctuality wasn't the only lesson Uncle Bobby drilled into me that I used to help me advance in my career. I have him to thank for many life lessons that he instilled in me while I lived with him. It was for only eighteen months, between the ages of fourteen and fifteen and a half, but it changed the direction of my life.

Where my father fell short as my role model, Uncle Bobby rose to the occasion. He was the opposite of his brother in every way. Where my father was dealing drugs and women, Uncle Bobby was going to church and devoting his life to God. Before Uncle Bobby came into my life, I never had any type of relationship with God. Living with my uncle, I had Bible study on Tuesdays and Thursdays, and we went to church on Sunday. He was adamant that I had to take part, too. I had to know scripture; I had to be able to answer questions and recite passages in my Bible study sessions.

Uncle Bobby also taught me about consequences. The previous year, the one when my dad was in England, no one cared if I got into trouble. But living with Uncle Bobby, someone cared about my behavior—and getting into trouble, especially with the law, wasn't an option with my uncle.

He even cared about how I took care of the things in my life. To this day, my wife laughs at me because I have to have everything in a certain place. And I always keep my shoes clean, shining them every morning before I slip them on. I learned this from Uncle Bobby, who took immaculate care of everything he owned and paid attention to how he presented himself to the world. He took a lot of pride in caring for his things and himself, and that stuck with me through the years, too.

There were so many lessons that I connect back to Uncle Bobby. He was the person who brought structure into my life and showed me discipline and how to follow through with your words and actions. If you say you're going to do something, then you are going to do it right, according to Uncle Bobby.

I remember the first report card I received when living with Uncle Bobby; it was Cs, Ds, and Fs. "Go upstairs. Take off all your clothes. Leave your underwear on," Uncle Bobby said. I thought, *What the hell?* I get upstairs, and Uncle Bobby had this leather strap that he used to whip my ass.

Afterward, I stood sobbing. He said to me, "Son, what do you want?" I stared at him blankly, not comprehending what he meant. "Son, in this house, you have to work hard, and you have to get good grades." He looked at me, and without raising his voice, he asked me again, "What do you want?"

Until that moment, no one had ever asked me what I wanted. I still had no idea how to answer his question, so I asked him what he meant. Again, he said, "What do you want? I'm not expecting you to come in the house with straight As, but I am expecting you to come in with Bs and Cs and to work hard."

"OK." I nodded.

"If you bring in Bs and Cs, what do you want, JeVon?"

I would get something for working hard? Well, OK. I know what I want.

This was around 1984–1985, and Michael Jordan had exploded in the NBA. Like most fourteen-year-old boys, I wanted a pair of Air Jordans.

When I was a kid living with my mom, I had always wanted a pair of red Converse sneakers. My mom didn't have the money. She could get me two pairs of shoes for the price of one, so I had the two cheaper pairs. It didn't stop me from asking for those Converse, and she would tell me,

"When you can buy your own shoes, JeVon, you can buy any shoes you want, as many as you want." My closet today is a combination of Neiman Marcus and Footlocker. I have more shoes than my wife.

I told Uncle Bobby I wanted a pair of the new Air Jordans. Uncle Bobby told me that if I brought in Bs and Cs, he'd buy me the Air Jordans that I wanted.

The next semester, I worked my ass off and applied myself to my studies the best I could. I got my report card back, and it was all Bs and Cs. I beamed with pride. It was the first time I had applied myself in school.

I sat on Uncle Bobby's porch, gripping the report card in my hand and fidgeting, antsy for him to come home from work. As soon as he pulled into the driveway, I ran over to greet him. "Uncle Bobby! Uncle Bobby!" I thrust the report card at him. He skimmed it, nodding his head. "Oh, good job, JeVon. Good job." Then he walked into the house without another word to me.

A little while later, he said he needed to run to the mall to pick up a few things. Not once did he mention the Air Jordans. As we drove to the mall, I thought, *You said you'd buy me the Air Jordans. What the hell?* However, I didn't want to push the envelope with him.

We got to the mall and started walking past the stores. I could see the Footlocker sign, and I got excited. But then, we walked by. We ran his errands, but he never said a word about the shoes. I was dejected.

Then, after all his errands were done, we walked by Footlocker once more. Uncle Bobby stopped. "Well, is this the place?" he asked me. I nodded my head as fast as I could. "Well, all right, then. Tell the man what you want."

Growing up with my father's broken promises, I honestly didn't know what to do or how to think about this. Uncle Bobby came through. He kept his word to me. Not that my mom didn't follow through, but I had never been in this situation until that day, where if I produced something, I got something in return.

I told the sales clerk that I wanted a pair of Air Jordans. I asked for the original black and reds. He measured my feet, walked to the back, brought out a box, and handed it to me.

I opened the box slowly, like it was the Ark of the Covenant. I reached down, pulled one out, and examined it. For some reason, I smelled it. It smelled like nothing I'd ever smelled. It smelled of rubber and leather and newness. I put them on. They fit perfectly, and I refused to take them off. I wore them out of the store. I think I even slept in them.

Getting those Air Jordans was life changing for me. I felt unstoppable. I thought to myself, *This is what it's like to have someone come through for you. This is what it's like to work hard and get the reward.*

I knew well the heartbreak and disappointment that comes when someone you trust breaks their word. In fact, that was my entire world. It was the only thing I knew.

But then, along came my Uncle Bobby, who followed through on what he said. He showed me a different world, a different way to be. He showed me that I could live in a world like his. He taught me to believe that that world could be mine if I worked for it.

This moment also taught me that it was possible to work hard and get rewarded. And it showed me how important it is that if you say something, you have to do it. Your word matters, and it does make a difference in a person's life.

For the rest of my life, I vowed to keep my word and work hard—just like Uncle Bobby.

* * *

Uncle Bobby was strict on discipline and work ethic, and he believed in having good manners, too. When I first lived with him and my aunt, he would call my name, and like most teenage boys, I'd shout back, "Yeah?" or "Huh?"

That was *not* the right response.

His eyebrows would rise to his hairline, his neck muscles would tighten, and he'd snap out, *"Excuse me?"* Uncle Bobby would get angry, and I knew I had messed up.

I needed to learn the rules of engagement with Uncle Bobby, fast. Rule number one: if he called you, you answered and you didn't yell. Your only response was to say, "Coming!" Once you stood in front of him, then you said, "Yes, sir."

Saying "sir" and "ma'am" was a must. It didn't matter whom you spoke with; it was always, "Thank you, ma'am," or, "Thank you, sir." I didn't realize it at the time, but learning to speak respectfully and to display good manners would be one of the tools that helped me to rise in the business world. It is the language of commerce and enabled me to be taken seriously by people. Even today, in every interaction, whether it's in person or an email or a note that I send on Slack, I end it with a "Thank you, ma'am," or, "Thank you, sir."

This is one of the biggest rules of society. There is a specific language spoken in the business world, and if you want to succeed, if you want to win the game, you need to learn that language. It's part of the rules of the game. You need to learn how to speak to fit into the environment.

Thank God Uncle Bobby was there to teach me this skill.

*   *   *

Uncle Bobby walked the straight and narrow path. He went to work every morning at the same time and came home at the same time every night. He had a hobby—golf. He went to church. He took care of his family. He was structured and disciplined with me, my cousins, and his grandson. If your chore was washing dishes or cutting grass that week, you better be sure you completed your chore. And he owned rental homes, and my cousins, some of my brothers, and I were the cleaning crew.

Many of his rental units were Section 8 housing. This was during a time when there weren't standards for how renters cared for the property. When tenants were evicted, moved, or just stopped showing up, we'd go to clean the place. God, it was like walking into an episode of *Ghetto Hoarders*. The people who leased my uncle's duplexes were filthy. They trashed his places. When you lifted a couch cushion or scooted a chair away from the wall, you had no idea what was hiding. Rats and roaches would scurry by. We'd find rotten diapers.

It would take us six or seven hours to clean the place, and when we finished, he'd slap two or three dollars into our hands. For a second, I'd stare at that money, thinking, *Seriously? All that work and this is all I get?*

But then my mindset would shift, and I'd immediately think, "OK, Uncle Bobby gave me three dollars. Well, I can turn it into six dollars." (This was my dad's hustler ways coming through.)

I would take the money Uncle Bobby had given to me, and I'd try to double it by shooting dice, playing cards, or pitching quarters with the other boys on the playground. Pitching quarters is a game where you and an opponent stand back and throw quarters toward the wall. Whoever gets closest to the wall wins all the quarters. I always had the same goal: to double my money. One day, I turned two dollars into thirty-five dollars.

This mindset, of taking what I have and making it better, remains with me today. My mom asked what I would do if I won $100 million. "Invest it and turn it into $200 million," I replied.

Just as I believe things can always get better for me, I'm always looking for ways to make that happen. To me, it's about looking to create opportunities in life. Pitching quarters or playing cards or dice was just the opportunity I had at that moment in my life to increase my wealth. Now, instead of gambling, I invest. Investing is a game you can consistently win. In gambling, the house always wins, so if you aren't the house, gambling is a bad investment.

Living with Uncle Bobby, under his guidance and structure, I began to see the different options and paths in life. Before Uncle Bobby, I was simply surviving, trying to live day to day with no plan, guidance, or structure. Hell, I never believed I'd live to see the age of twenty-five. I didn't know corporate America existed. I didn't know anything about being a leader or making an honest living. Sure, I knew from a young age that I didn't want to be like my father; I didn't want to go down his road. Nevertheless, I wasn't sure what else existed. I didn't know what I didn't know.

But with a little direction, discipline, and tough love from Uncle Bobby, I got to see a different future for myself. I spent eighteen months living and learning under Uncle Bobby's care, and I saw how another man made a living in the world—an honest living.

Those eighteen months were the most impactful, life-altering days of my life. It changed how I viewed the world. It changed how I behaved in the world. It changed how I understood the world.

I still don't know why he agreed to take me in. I don't know what changed between that first time I ran away after caring for my brother and sisters for three weeks and his refusing to take me in. He had car payments, a home, three kids, and his grandson living with him, yet he took on another mouth to feed.

But I thank God every day for Uncle Bobby. He was exactly what I needed at that age, at that impressionable point in my life. I don't know where or what my life would look like if he had said no.

From my mom, I learned the grinding attitude. *Never quit, always keep going, do the right thing.*

From my father, I learned how to hustle. *Be nice to everyone, take risks.*

Uncle Bobby appeared in my life and helped create a bridge between the worlds and lessons of my mother and father. He brought discipline, maturity, manners, and work ethic into my life. In a way, he taught me how to unite the *vision* of my father with the *execution* of my mother and place it in the context of the broader world.

I will be forever grateful to this man for his role in helping me to develop a formula of success.

A NEW PATH

While living with Uncle Bobby, I learned that my father wanted me to come live with him again. It was an odd request. *Why?* I thought. *You never took care of me in the first damn place. Why would you want me to come back to live with you?* Everything was great with Uncle Bobby.

I thought, *Here we go again.* Just when I believed everything in my life was starting to go well for me, it seemed like all hell was about to break loose again. It felt like I couldn't catch a break, or at least, the breaks didn't last for me.

I was devastated, thinking that I was about to go back to living with my father and his horrific girlfriends and lifestyle.

I told Uncle Bobby I didn't want to go back. I was happy with him. I was getting good grades in school. I had my Air Jordans. Life was good.

"I'll talk to him, but I can't keep you from your father if he wants you," was all Uncle Bobby would say on the subject.

I was anxious and afraid, not just because I didn't want to live with Amber, but I was also terrified that my dad would rip me away from Uncle Bobby's only to leave me alone again.

About a month after the news that my father wanted me

back, Uncle Bobby told me to pack my mom's raggedy suitcase. I thought for sure he was bringing me to my dad's. But instead, he brought me to the airport.

There, he handed me a one-way ticket to Texas to be with my mom.

I always thought it was my Uncle Bobby who bought my plane ticket and sent me to live with my mom. But it wasn't. It was my mom—a truth I didn't learn until I was in my mid-forties.

When my dad started telling Uncle Bobby that he wanted me to go back and live with him, Uncle Bobby called my mom and told her what my dad was trying to do. Although she was saving money to bring me to Texas, my dad's attempt to get me back forced her to do it immediately.

This meant she took loans out from friends, worked extra shifts, picked up extra jobs, and scraped together everything she could to bring me home to her.

Few moments in my life have left more joy and gratitude in my heart than learning the truth. My mom came back for me. She never forgot about me. In the end, my mom saved me. My protector, the woman who loved me the most, came and plucked me out of Dayton and saved me from a life on the streets.

That day, I sat on the plane with my mom's old, tattered suitcase stuffed under the seat in front of me. I was fifteen, ready to start my sophomore year and a new life.

To this day, outside of getting married and having children, getting out of Dayton to reunite with my mom when I was fifteen was the greatest thing that ever happened to me. Leaving Dayton was leaving the pimp, drug dealer lifestyle behind. It was leaving the path that would have taken me to man prison or ended with me dead from a gunshot or a stabbing.

When you grow up in my father's world in the hood, you have three paths to making money. The first is as a drug dealer or pimp, but that road leaves you in prison or behind bars. You've never met a retired drug dealer, pimp, or hustler, who made so much money that he could retire, get out of the game, and live happily ever after. That doesn't exist.

The second path off the streets and earning good money is through sports. Kids see successful basketball players like LeBron James who grew up on the streets of Akron, Ohio, so they go to the park, they hustle, and play ball. However, only a small fraction of those kids make it in professional sports.

The third path is through music—rap, in particular. Just

like with the athletes, the kids see a rapper and they want to be that person, so they go after the beat.

Most kids from the streets have no idea that a fourth path exists—business. They have no clue that they can succeed in business because this option doesn't exist in their world.

But by the grace of God, that fourth path was unveiled to me by Uncle Bobby. And it became an option once I was reunited with my mom in Texas. I'm convinced that had I stayed in Dayton, I would have followed in my father's footsteps or worse.

I still feel guilty about everyone I left behind. Many of my half brothers and half sisters never got out, and many still live there, caught in the same destructive cycle that we grew up in. My heart aches for them, for the lives that never were.

My heart aches for all the boys and girls who never get out, who never come to know the fourth path, the path of business, exists.

My heart also aches because I'm ashamed. I'm ashamed that I'm happy to be out. That could have been me. It should have been me. If not for Uncle Bobby and my mom, it would have been me.

Cleaning Toilets

————

BY THE TIME I WAS BACK WITH MOM, SHE HAD MOVED from Houston to San Antonio. We upgraded from a tiny apartment to a rental house in a decent neighborhood. I made friends with a kid named Jeff and his brother Steven who lived down the street, and we often played at their house.

I had never seen anything like their home before. Jeff and his brother each had their own Nintendo system and a television in their rooms. Then there was a big television in the living room, a dog, and a cockatoo. I would spin in a circle gazing at all their stuff, thinking, *Man, these guys are living the dream.*

One day when we were playing video games, Jeff's mom asked us if we wanted pizza.

"Anything in particular you would like on your pizza, JeVon?"

No one had ever asked me what I wanted on my pizza. When I ate pizza in Dayton, I was just happy to snag a slice. "No, ma'am," I replied, just as Uncle Bobby always taught me. "I'm willing to eat whatever you all want."

"OK, we'll get two pizzas."

Damn, we're getting two pizzas? I thought. *Where am I?*

We went back to playing video games when I heard the doorbell ring. I was waiting for my turn, so their mom asked if I could answer the door. "Yes, ma'am." I hopped up from the floor and went to the door.

What greeted me on the other side was something I had never witnessed: a young boy stood there holding two pizzas in cardboard boxes.

"Yes, sir?" I asked him.

"I have your pizzas."

I stared blankly at the boy, not comprehending what was happening on the doorstep. Who was this guy and what was he doing carrying pizza? Leaving the door open, I turned and walked back into the house. "Someone's here," I said to the boys' mother.

She walked to the door, asked how much it cost, and handed the delivery boy the money, who then passed two pizzas and two bottles of soda (different flavors, too!) to her. I stood off to the side absorbing the scene in front of me.

The mother breezed by me, hardly sparing me a glance as I fell in line behind her. I watched her walk into the kitchen, set the pizzas down, grab paper plates, and then open the boxes. A little waft of steam escaped.

"So, they bring the pizza to you?" I asked, confused by what I was witnessing.

Three sets of eyes locked onto me. "Huh?" Jeff asked, himself confused by my demeanor.

"Why did they bring the pizza here? Why didn't we have to go and pick it up?" I was trying to make sense of this odd event.

"Well, JeVon, we ordered delivery," the mom said to me

patiently. But by now she was looking at me, almost dumb-founded that she had to explain the inner workings of pizza delivery to me—as if I should just know it because everyone orders pizza for delivery, right?

But I was still connecting the dots. "OK, wait a minute," I said. "You called the pizza place, and they brought it here, to the house, and you just take it from them?"

"Yes."

It was making sense to me now. "Wow! That is *so* cool!" I was delighted with this new knowledge. Who the hell had ever heard of someone bringing food to you?

"Wait, you've never ordered pizza?" Jeff and Steven's mom asked, as though she was trying to connect the dots on my strange behavior.

"No, but it's pretty awesome!" I said, grinning. "I'll be right back," I called as I spun on my heel and went to gather my stuff.

"Wait, where are you going?" everyone called as I made my way to the front door.

"I got to go tell my mom about this!" I yelled.

I was too excited to eat. As a fifteen-year-old kid, this was one of the most amazing things I had ever learned. When I was in Dayton, there was no pizza delivery, at least, not with the people I lived with.

I jogged down the street and burst through the front door. "Mom! Mom! Did you know you can order pizza and they'll bring it to you?" I shouted as soon as I crossed the threshold, not waiting to see where she was. I was like a five-year-old kid excited for Santa Claus. Mom came around the corner and laughed when she saw the look on my face. She gave me a small hug and tiny smile. "That's great, JeVon."

Maybe she already knew the wonders of pizza delivery, but if she did, she never let on. Instead, Mom let me have my moment of unadulterated joy.

* * *

There's a phrase in Zen Buddhism called "beginner's mind." It's a state where a person is open, eager, and without any pre-conceived notions when learning something for the first time.

I was the living embodiment of the beginner's mind when I first arrived in San Antonio, mainly because I was a beginner in this world. My mom had landed us smack-dab in middle-class suburbia, which could have been Africa for all I knew or understood.

The normal rituals of middle-class American life, like order-
ing pizza delivery, were new to me. These are things that
most people take for granted, but none of these were parts
of my life before.

Most of us walk into our kitchens and flip a light switch
expecting the overhead lightbulb to click on. But what if
nothing came on because you didn't have the money to
pay the electricity bill? Or your landlord is too cheap to
fix the electrical outlet? How many of us open the refrigerator door expecting the shelves to be stocked with food?
If you peeked in my pantry today, you'd see food stacked
on top of food.

Until I lived with Uncle Bobby, a lot of the things most
people take for granted were absent in my life. When I
lived with Uncle Bobby, I caught glimpses of this world, of
what a different life could be from what I had experienced
living with my mom and off and on with my dad. But I still
wasn't exposed to the middle- and upper-middle classes
that existed for many Americans. San Antonio was like a
secret world that I was granted entry into—a world where
the lights always came on, where pizza came to your doorstep, and where you could play outside without watching
a drug deal go down.

Even my high school was unlike anything I had seen before.

It was about 2,500 students, most of them white, with Hispanics and blacks making up a very small minority. This was new to me. I had never been around that many white kids before.

And then there was PE. The first time I walked out of the gymnasium toward the playing fields, I was taken aback by this noise, "MOOOOOOO!"

"What the hell is that?" I said to my friends walking next to me.

I saw this giant brown thing—a building—in the middle of the field.

"Oh, that's the FFA barn."

"What the hell is FFA?"

The kids started laughing. "You don't know what FFA is?" they said, as if my comment was the most ridiculous thing they'd ever heard. How was it possible for me to *not* know what FFA stood for?

"No, what is it?"

"It's the Future Farmers of America, where they learn about

raising and caring for animals," one boy explained. "It's a class people take to become a farmer."

Farmers? Animals? I heard the words, but they weren't computing. I grew up surrounded by concrete and cement, not fields or animals. What my friends were explaining made no sense to me.

My friends saw my confusion and suggested we walk over to check it out. They brought me to the Ag Barn, which was the giant building I had seen when I first started walking to the field. They opened the doors, and there were bulls, sheep, chickens, and cattle.

It was like I had stepped onto Noah's Ark.

"Wow, you guys have a petting zoo at the school! This is cool!"

My friends looked at one another. "Uh, this isn't a petting zoo; it's FFA."

"Nah," I said, shaking my head, "this is a petting zoo."

I still didn't understand what FFA or farming meant. But they had real, live animals that I could reach out and touch. In the world that I came from, that was a petting zoo.

Life in San Antonio was, without a doubt, better than life in Dayton. But this also meant I had to adjust to the suburban life and lifestyles of my friends who were in the middle to upper-middle classes. I grew up in a different world from them. Even though life was now better, I still felt like an outsider.

And I still had a lot to learn about how people in this class lived.

Some of my friends came from homes where the parents were well-off. Mom and Dad both worked, or Dad worked and Mom stayed home watching the kids. I would go to their homes for dinner, and the parents and the kids would sit around the table, *talking,* having real conversations about their days with one another.

I even saw some kids talk back to their parents, which was wild to me. I knew nothing about how to live like this. Sure, Uncle Bobby gave me a small taste of this life, but even that was different. I mean, Uncle Bobby was a man who *left* his family at home to go on a church vacation without them because they weren't at the van at ten sharp.

Sometimes it was hard to understand what I was observing. The same way it was difficult for me to understand *The*

Brady Bunch. Watching that show on television and seeing a mom, a dad, six kids, a maid, a dog, and a cat living in a beautiful home with two cars made no sense to me. On top of that, the mom didn't work!

Do people really *live like that?* I would think.

When I watched the show *Good Times* about a black family who rented an apartment in the hood, I understood that perfectly. On the show, the elevator was always broken in their building, they struggled to make ends meet, and they had three kids in a two-bedroom place. I related to that lifestyle. But in San Antonio, I couldn't relate, and it was hard to fit in. I felt like I had landed in an episode of *The Brady Bunch.*

My best friend in San Antonio, Bishop, who remains my best friend in the world today, was a guy like me. His dad had passed away in a car wreck. His mom was like my mom. She worked her tail off all the time trying to care for him and his brother. We became friends because we understood each other; we understood the other side of life that many of the kids in the part of San Antonio where we lived couldn't comprehend.

It wasn't just the home lives these kids lived that perplexed me. It was what they did for fun that I had to adjust to as well. I came from the land of welfare, heroin, drug addicts, pimps, hookers, whores, and prostitutes; it was the bottom of the barrel.

Even though that stuff was around me, I never smoked weed. I never did coke. I never did heroin, and I never drank alcohol. But when I got to San Antonio, some of the suburban kids whom I befriended took me to parties on the weekend. "Oh, Chris is having a two-kegger," they'd say. "A two-kegger?" I'd ask. "What's that?"

"Oh, that's a party with two kegs of beer," they'd explain.

"Uh, what's a keg?"

I didn't know what these things were, and the first party I went to stunned me. All these kids were drinking—for fun—in this nice house. My head whipped from wall to wall watching drunk teenagers stumble and get sloppy. All I could think about was how disrespectful they were being in this house. Uncle Bobby taught me well. I was offended, and it wasn't even my home.

I didn't understand drinking for recreation and fun. These kids had nice cars, money in their pockets, and credit cards, courtesy of Mom and Dad to use on their whims. Partying was a way for them to have fun.

But where I came from, what I saw growing up, people drank or used drugs because they were addicts. It wasn't fun for them. It wasn't to relax and have a good time. It was to escape the hell they were living in, to forget their pain and trauma. They used these substances because they didn't know how to stop; they had no other way out of their lives.

When my friends found out that I'd never tasted alcohol, they got excited. "Oh, my God! We're getting you drunk!" they shouted.

I went along with them, thinking, *Why not?* But I had no clue what alcohol did to your body or how it messed you up. I drank what they put in my hand. I had about eight Coors Lights, and then I swigged Jack Daniel's straight out of the bottle. About an hour or so into my "fun," life got real for me. I threw up everywhere. It was horrific.

Everyone told me I would have a hangover the next day. I wasn't sure what they meant or what it would feel like, and honestly, I still don't. What happened to me was not a hangover. I woke up with a painful physical reminder of what my childhood was like. It was the same feeling I used to get when I woke up after going to bed without dinner because we couldn't afford food. It was a gnawing, a clawing, in my stomach. There's nothing fun about that feeling.

Even thinking about it now, the memory sickens me. After waking up with my first hangover, I vowed no drugs or alcohol for me. If this feeling was the result of recreational partying, then I wanted no part of it.

And that's a commitment I've kept. To this day, I don't drink or do drugs. They are a too-painful reminder of where I came from—and not the good parts.

GRADUATING FROM HIGH SCHOOL

Being back with Mom meant being back with my protector. Life was good. I had consistency and structure again. I was with the one person who loved me more than anyone else in the world. But that didn't mean everything was perfect in San Antonio. Mom and I hadn't lived together for five years. A lot changes from the ages of ten to fifteen. We had our strains, as any parent-child relationship would under normal circumstances, and we had to find a new rhythm of relating and living together again.

But I was back with my mom once more, and that's all that mattered. I had a hug and an "I love you" given to me every night before I went to bed.

Of course, celebrating Christmas was a highlight for me. We had a Christmas tree and lights, and I remember how much fun I had decorating the tree during our first holi-day together. I hadn't celebrated Christmas in five years. My dad and his girlfriends never bought me anything or decorated a tree, and Uncle Bobby was a Jehovah's Witness, and they don't recognize or celebrate Christmas, birthdays, or any holidays.

Uncle Bobby would say to me, "We don't celebrate Christmas. We choose to do for one another as a family all year long." That hit me hard. I love the lights and decorations, the movies, and the shopping. And now that I have kids, I love watching them enjoy the holiday. But I like Uncle Bobby's perspective too. And I try to live by that creed throughout the year.

I remember my first Christmas back with my mom; she had a full hysterectomy after Thanksgiving. Before the surgery, she worked overtime so she could buy Christmas lights to hang outside our home. After the surgery, she was supposed to take it easy and not exert herself while she recovered. But nothing was going to stop my mom from making Christmas a great holiday for me.

Days after her operation, I found her climbing a ladder to hang the colored lights on the house. She was doing this all for me because she remembered how much I loved Christmas when I was a kid. She ignored her doctor's orders all so I could smile.

Then there was the Christmas season when she worked overtime so she could buy me the $35 Coca-Cola shirt that I wanted. Those shirts were popular back in the 1980s.

Even in San Antonio, Mom worked hard to make everything bigger and better, never quitting, just to ensure that I enjoyed some simple pleasures—pleasures that many middle- to upper-middle-class Americans take for granted.

Life with Mom was tame, almost boring, compared to my previous life. But Mom was still in survival mode. I didn't have a Nintendo or a personal television in my bedroom. I wasn't driving a fancy car or whipping out a credit card like many of my classmates. Mom was working hard to put food on the table, to pay the rent, and to keep the lights on for us.

If her job was to bring in the money, then my job was to go to school and do my schoolwork. There was just one problem with this equation. The Dayton school system pushed me through, which meant, academically, I wasn't where I should be. I was far behind in math, reading, science, and just about every subject.

At the beginning of the school year, my mom and I met with the guidance counselor to enroll me in the tenth grade. He asked me for the name of the last math class I had taken at my old school. I had no idea.

"Well, in tenth grade, you should be on the level of geometry," he said.

Without breaking eye contact with the guidance counselor, I nodded affirmatively and said, "OK." This was the first time I'd ever heard the word *geometry*. My mindset was, "OK, they're going to put me in geometry. I'm going to go in this class. I'm going to sit and I'm going to listen and I'm going to learn. I will accomplish it."

I had the drive, I had the desire, but I damn sure didn't have the foundation to do it. I was put in geometry, I showed up, but I had no clue what was going on. I was lost in geometry and in all my classes. After about six weeks and an abysmal report, everyone knew I needed to go back and take remedial classes. This meant I was stuck at the end of the hall, where the "dumb" kids went.

Because Mom was still in survival mode, she worked a lot and took as much overtime as she could to keep the money flowing. However, this also meant she wasn't around to help me with homework after school. That said, even if she'd been there, I'm not sure she could have guided me. My mom struggled with school herself, having been pushed through the education system in the orphanage. Growing up, my mom's lessons were in how to sew, iron, cook, and clean—in other words, homemaking types of classes. Of course, she taught me all those skills like ironing, sewing, cooking, and cleaning, too, but those don't help with geometry.

Uncle Bobby was the first person in my life to push the importance of school. But Uncle Bobby never expected much from me. "Don't get an F or a D," he'd say, when his kids dealt in straight As. Straight As were the standard for my cousins. My standard was set much lower, and I knew it.

And it sucked knowing that people expected little from me. It gnawed at me. I knew I could do better.

Still, I struggled throughout high school. My senior year, when most kids were taking college-level courses, I was in the remedial ones. To give you a sense of how far behind I was in school, the second half of my senior year, I was just taking pre-algebra. I was still mastering how to add, subtract, and multiply numbers.

I struggled so much that I never graduated. I didn't get to walk with my classmates across the stage and receive my diploma. I never saw my mom beam with pride as I wore my cap and gown and sat in the uncomfortable chairs listening to the valedictorian's speech.

When I learned I wasn't going to graduate with my class, I was frustrated. I thought I owed my mom the chance to see me walk the stage and pick up my diploma. She had worked hard to take care of me, to feed me, and to give me a great life in San Antonio. I felt like I had let her down, that I was a disappointment. I figured I'd get a stern lecture from her when she learned the truth. However, she wasn't mad and no lecture came.

Instead, she gave me an ultimatum. I had two weeks to get a job while I went to summer school, or to get out of the house.

Her words shook me. There was my security blanket talking to me in a way that she'd never spoken to me before. So, in addition to going to summer school, I worked in the evenings.

I had three classes that I needed to complete in order to get my diploma. One of those classes was English, and thank God for my teacher. Part of the curriculum was a field trip to see the movie *Batman* and then to write an essay on it. That I could handle.

When I learned that I had passed my classes, I wanted my diploma. Straightaway, I took the certificate showing that I passed to my high school front office. I didn't have any specific expectations for what the school would say or do, but the other kids had a big celebration, they walked the stage and people clapped. I thought something cool would happen for me, too.

My first surprise came when I walked into my school. It was empty. I looked around and headed to the main office, expecting to see the secretaries and assistants. Instead, the only person I found sitting at the front desk was the janitor.

"What can I do for you?" he asked gruffly.

"Uh, I need to pick up my high school diploma," I said. "Here's the certificate stating I passed everything." I held out the paper for him while I sported a huge grin. My eyes darted around the room, wondering what was going to happen. Scrunching his eyes, he looked at my paper, and then told me he'd be right back. I watched him talk to a lady in the back. She skimmed the papers, nodded her head, and I saw him mouth "yes."

Then the janitor walked to a safe, unlocked it, and took out a piece of paper. "Here you go." He shoved it at me. I stared dumbly for a moment, then took the flimsy sheet of paper from him and muttered a tiny, "Thank you, sir." He turned away from me and started walking back into the offices, as though he had better things to do than hand an eighteen-year-old kid his diploma.

I looked at the sheet of paper and then around the room,

still waiting for something, for anything, to happen. But nothing did. I didn't even get a "congratulations" from the janitor. I don't know what I was waiting for, like did I expect confetti to suddenly pour down or for someone to run up and offer me a job? No.

But then again, I didn't think I would get my high school diploma from the school janitor.

INTO THE WORKING WORLD

As soon as the janitor handed me the diploma and I was an official high school graduate, Mom told me it was time to get a real job—not some part-time, happy little gig but a serious, grown-man job.

Mom wasn't messing around, and she wasn't about to help me. It was up to me to find a job. So I went from restaurant to restaurant asking for applications. Eventually, a restaurant called Po Folks hired me. To this day, I shake my head in wonder over the name; I mean, Mom and I were the living, breathing definition of "po folks."

I worked as a busboy from nine in the morning to three in the afternoon every day. We had one car between us, so I would drop Mom off at work, drive to my job, then pick her up when her day ended.

As soon as I walked through the doors at Po Folks, I headed for the restrooms. My first order of business was to clean them from the night before, then I would make iced tea, and then I would bus tables until my shift ended. I kept my restrooms immaculate, the way Uncle Bobby kept his home and possessions. To this day, I'm certain that the cleanest toilets and nicest tables in all of San Antonio were at my Po Folks.

Everything shone under my care, from the spoons to the salt and pepper shakers, from the chairs to the tables. I never wanted my customers to sit at one of my tables and have to wipe crumbs from a seat or to mop up a spill left from the last diners.

I would think back to my childhood while working at Po Folks, and it put everything about my job in perspective. Were the restrooms dirty from the night before? Sure, but even at their dirtiest, they were nothing compared to the filth and stench I had to deal with when cleaning Uncle Bobby's rental units. The dirtiest night left the restroom sparkling compared to some of the places I had to clean.

Even busing tables was an easy job to swallow. Busing and cleaning tables wasn't hard work for a boy who grew up putting bread bags on his feet and walking to the store to run errands in the rain or snow because Mom didn't have thirty-five cents to ride the bus.

All the struggles I endured in my past—the beatings, sleeping at the bus stop, doing time in juvenile detention—ignited a spark inside of me that drove me to work as hard as possible at Po Folks. This job may not have been glamorous, but it was a way out. I was eighteen, a grown man, and I had to find a way to make a living—and I had to do it the legal way. I was determined to live a different life than my father.

Even though I was cleaning toilets and tables, and I was the lowest man on the totem pole, I busted my ass and took pride in every single responsibility I had. I took pride in how clean the restrooms were. I took pride in making the iced tea. I took pride in the tables I bused. I was proud when the cooks grabbed one of the dishes I cleaned to plate the food that they never had to bark at me, "Hey, the plates aren't clean."

I took pride in the job and in myself. I didn't care about my job title. I cared about the quality of my efforts and the work ethic I brought to my job. This was the beginning of an attitude that I have carried with me to this day. It's the mentality that says, "OK, whatever I do in this world, I'm going to be the best. And if my job right now is to clean toilets, then so be it. I'm going to be the best toilet cleaner in the damn city."

It was like when Uncle Bobby spoke to me about my grades.

He told me he expected me to work hard and do the best that I could. Those lessons I took to heart, and I applied them at Po Folks. In fact, I've approached every job in my life with those lessons.

My efforts at Po Folks didn't go unnoticed. Often, my manager would say to me, "You're the best employee I have ever had," or, "I've never seen someone take so much pride in their work." Her praise made me feel good about myself and my work. And I loved that she got to the point where she stopped checking the bathrooms because she knew they sparkled.

While I was at Po Folks, I also enrolled (at my mother's encouragement) at San Antonio College, a community college. I went to school at night and on the weekends. School was still hard. I was still taking remedial classes that weren't eligible for college credit and having to pay for them on top of it. I ended up stopping after a few semesters.

I may grumble about taking community college classes, but I'm glad I went. Taking classes and working full time reinforced my hustle and work ethic. This period was a catalyst in helping me create my current view of life. I realized I wanted more than to work low-paying jobs. I didn't want to clean toilets for the rest of my days. My friends were in college, enrolled in prestigious universities like Texas A&M

and the University of Texas, working toward their futures. I may not have been able to go to colleges like my friends, but I still wanted to succeed.

I needed to start working on my future, too. I needed to start playing the game of life for real.

When I look at where I am today in business, it all began at Po Folks. That was the moment when I pulled together the lessons I learned from my father, mother, and Uncle Bobby in a positive way to help me make it in the legal world.

SEVEN

Playing the
Game for Real

———

WHEN YOU WORK HARD AND GET RESULTS IN YOUR JOB,
eventually the right people notice. My commitment to the
most sparkling bathrooms and the cleanest tables at Po
Folks restaurant got me noticed by one of the regulars—a
family who owned a candle shop at the mall. They offered
me a job in their store. It paid one dollar more than what
I was making at the restaurant, so I took it.

The husband-and-wife team taught me how to make candles. It was a cool job for a teenager in the late 1980s and
early 1990s. The store had a giant glass window display. I
would sit behind the window and make candles while all
the girls walked by.

Mom was working at Nationwide Insurance at the time, and she saw that I was putting in real effort into my jobs. When a position opened up in her company, she asked if I was interested. I would collect and pass out the mail, and I'd work in the records department filing. It wasn't much, but it was a start, so I figured why not.

Mom took me to buy a nice outfit for my interview. It was my first pair of dress slacks, a button-up shirt, and tie. I had no idea how to tie a tie and neither did Mom, so I had to ask the neighbor to teach me (no YouTube at this time).

I nailed the interview and they offered me the job. Nationwide Insurance was one of the biggest insurance companies in the country, and this was my first look inside a real office in corporate America. Working in the mailroom let me see every department, and it was the perfect position for me to observe the workings of a large corporation from different angles.

What I saw blew me away. Over the course of the day, I watched and learned, studying how people acted, their behaviors, their mannerisms, whom they spent time with, and who climbed the corporate ladder. And I started to learn about office politics.

Being observant is a valuable tool. It served me well growing up in Dayton, watching my mom, my father, and Uncle Bobby, and it served me well as I embarked on my professional career.

This isn't manipulation; for me, it's a survival instinct. Being acutely aware of everything going on around you is a luxury for someone who came from a good home. It's a necessity for someone who did not.

Coming from such chaotic and violent homes, I had to be aware of what everyone was thinking, and where I stood in relation to them. Whether I ate or not and whether I slept in a bed or not were often determined by my ability to properly read the adults around me.

Even now, when I walk into a room, I make note of how many people there are, who says what, and what's happening at any given moment. And then I match and mirror them. I don't imitate; I just reflect their energy and attitude back on them. I see who they are, get a gauge on them before I reveal who I am, and then I reveal only what I need to succeed.

My job in the mailroom and filing papers was the moment when I started to see how to use these skills to maneuver in the world of work. Things clicked. Of course, I took the lessons of my past and used them to my benefit.

From day one, I said hello to everyone, just like my father taught me. I asked them how they were and smiled brightly at them. I always asked if there was more I could do to help, demonstrating the strong work ethic and discipline that Uncle Bobby showed me.

I took these lessons from the street and added to them based on what I was learning from observation. I remember one vice president would always say, "Tremendous!" when someone asked how he was doing. It didn't matter if he had a bad day, he was tremendous. If he had a phenomenal day, he was tremendous. This response meant no one knew what was going on with him, his mindset, his thoughts, or what he was calculating. I saw how people responded to him, with a smile, a wave, and a cheerful response. So I began to mimic him. When someone asked me how I was doing, I told them, "I'm excellent!" Even today, that is still my standard line, and it'll continue to be my standard line until the day I die.

I respond this way partly because I've learned, at the end of the day, life keeps going no matter what happens to us. Nothing stops. The day I learned that my father had passed away, bills still had to be paid, employees needed their checks, traffic jammed the streets of Austin, and my daughter and son needed a bath before bed. We have to keep going, just like my mom taught me, no matter what's happening around us. We can't crumble. We can't fold. So telling someone, "I'm excellent," when they ask is a way for me to keep going no matter what is happening.

While at Nationwide Insurance, I used my observation skills to see and learn the unspoken language and rituals of American business: how people shook hands; how they dressed in sharp suits, tidy ties, and neat shoes; and the words, the language, they used to speak with one another.

Oddly enough, the president of Nationwide was a black man. A black man! I thought my eyes were deceiving me. This was the first time I had seen a black man in a suit, and he was walking the halls of a company—leading the company, no less. The only black men I knew were pimps and drug dealers who spoke in slang. But at Nationwide, I saw the president dressed in clean, pressed suits. He spoke respectfully and articulately. He always smiled, and he looked people in the eye.

He mesmerized me. I memorized all his actions. I listened to the words he used, his intonation, his volume. I watched how he spoke, how he shook hands, and how he behaved so I could model my own behavior after him. I learned how to fit into the world of corporate America, of suits and ties, of power and money.

Working at Nationwide Insurance was another fork in

the road for me. It was the transformative experience I needed. It was the beginning of the vision of the fourth path I would take.

* * *

As soon as I got my job at Nationwide, Mom and I had a serious talk about our living arrangements. "OK, so here's a deal," she said. "If you're going to live here, I'm going to teach you what it's like to live."

OK, I thought, *but what does she mean?*

"You get paid twice a month," Mom said. "One of your checks you get to keep. The other check, you give it to me."

Without giving her any backtalk or attitude, I replied with a simple, "Yes, ma'am. OK." But Mom wasn't done teaching me about living yet. "And you're going to buy your own groceries. You're going to wash your own clothes. You're going to buy your own laundry detergent. You're going to learn what it's like to be self-sufficient."

When I lived with my dad and his girlfriends, I had to take care of my brothers and sisters, so I had a taste for what being self-sufficient meant. But as far as society is concerned—having a job, paying bills, and keeping your head above the poverty line—I had no clue how to do those things.

Like most things in my life, I learned by watching and doing. My mom taught me how to wash my clothes, which detergents to buy, and how to use them in the washer. She taught me how to budget my money, how to set aside money each week for groceries, gas, and other basic necessities. If I had money left over after those priorities, then I could spend a little pocket change on leisure and luxury items.

It didn't take me long to learn that if I gave one check to my mom, then I wasn't left with much for the month. I went into negotiation mode fast.

"Why don't I give you half of one check and half of the other?" I asked her. "That way, I have a consistent income."

She thought for a minute, then nodded in agreement. "That's fair," she said.

*   *   *

I learned a lot from my first job at Nationwide Insurance— how to walk, talk, and behave in corporate America. One of the greatest introductions I received was to personal finance and retirement planning.

Nationwide offered its employees Lunch & Learn Sessions as part of its commitment to developing its workers. One day, I walked by the conference room where the sessions were held, and I saw a sign that said, "Free Lunch." I had no idea what the topic was about, but a free lunch meant I could save money. So, of course I went to the session. Then the moment the instructor started talking, *boom!* I was hooked.

You mean I can give my money to someone, and they give me more back? This was when I fell in love with the world of investing, saving, and making money. It sounded like the greatest thing in the world.

That one session led me to make my first investment in a US Savings Bond—the absolute worst investments anyone can make. I remember putting $100 into a savings bond thinking I'll make a ton of money. Three years later, I think it was worth like $103. It was a horrible investment, so I got out of that and switched to learning about stocks.

But this was a game-changing moment for me. I saw how far—or rather, how little—the money I made in the mailroom took me. And I wanted more. I wanted to control the money like I did when I played Monopoly. Investing and learning how to invest was one avenue for me to achieve this goal. I went on to teach myself about investing and about the stock market, and it's worked out well for me.

It's ironic that my abilities with spreadsheets, revenue state-ments, and balance sheets have helped create my life. I could barely pass my high school math classes. I can't tell you the purpose of calculus; I probably couldn't spell it off the top of my head. However, I know how to deposit a check. I know how to make money. I know how to read profit and loss, income statements, and how to scale a company. And for the record, *both* the top and the bottom line matter. The true game of making money is built on the basics: addition, subtraction, multiplication, division, and percentages. If you know how to do those things, then you're good.

The real takeaway from this: society tells you that you need a lot of things, like trigonometry or a four-year college degree, to succeed. That's BS. You don't. You just need to figure out what matters to what you want. Trim the fat. Get rid of the trigonometry in your life and focus on what you're good at. Master the basics, and let the rest fall away.

* * *

I remember when I was in the mailroom at Nationwide Insurance, I stood shoulder to shoulder with a woman in her early thirties. She was married with a young daugh-ter. We both took home the same salary, about $10,000 a year. One day she pulled me aside. "You're going to get me fired," she said. *Huh?* I thought. I was confused. I was always respectful to her, never mean or disrespectful. In fact, I hardly spoke to her. I viewed her as my competition because she held the same job as me.

"How am I going to get you fired?" I asked.

"I can't keep up with you." She sighed. "I need this job. I have a daughter. I can't lose the benefits."

I was a kid myself, barely twenty years old, without any understanding of benefits and why she needed them. I paused when I heard her plea, but her words didn't make me stop or work less hard. It was like we were playing a game of Monopoly and she had asked me to let her win.

There's no letting people win in life; that isn't how life works. Society doesn't give you anything. An elite athlete like an NFL player doesn't go slower or take it easy on you so you can get a spot on the team. No, they go hard and fast, and they never stop. It's up to you to keep up with them, to play at their level, or find another outlet. If you want to improve your life, if you want to hit six figures, have a vice president's title after your name, or drive a Lexus, then you have to work for it. I was willing to work for it. If she didn't want to, that's fine, but I wasn't about to let her hold me back. If she wanted to get to my level, then that was on her. I wasn't going to lower myself so she could shine.

Looking back now, I'm a little remorseful for my response. Having my own family, I understand the need to protect and care for them. I understand her fear when she realized she couldn't keep pace with my work. There was a more emotionally mature way for me to deal with this, but I didn't have those skills then.

In fact, her words were like gasoline that turned my fire into a raging bonfire. They fueled me to push myself even more, to shine brighter than ever. I mean, I had been broke and hungry my whole life, and now here was this woman telling me not to reach for something great when it was right there in front of me.

I couldn't jeopardize my job. I couldn't let up. My work ethic and the need to outshine everyone around me stemmed from getting my hands on a little something in life. I had money in my pocket, a place to call my own, and a decent car to drive. I was a part of something, and I didn't want to lose that.

I couldn't go back to the life I endured as a child. I was making my way in the world without relying on public assistance or turning to the illegal underbelly of society for money. I climbed out of the hood. So what the woman asked of me was impossible for me to give her. That was my way to get noticed, a chance for me to create new opportunities for myself to move up through the ranks so I could make more money.

I was running from my childhood as fast and as far as possible. I couldn't stop for her.

MOVING UP

As a kid, my favorite meal was pork chops, mashed potatoes, and gravy. When I say pork chops, I'm not talking about the thick, butterfly pork chops. No, I'm talking about the $1.99 bone in, butt naked, thinly sliced ones. Cheap and filling, that's what mattered to my mom.

When I got the Nationwide Insurance job, my mom wanted to celebrate by making my favorite meal. I was thrilled. I made my mom proud of me. So we went to the grocery store for the ingredients. While standing in the checkout line, I saw *Flex* magazine and Lee Haney, the newly crowned Mr. Olympia, on the cover.

"Mom, will you get me this magazine?" I asked.

"You know what? You got the job. Yes, I'll get you the magazine."

I was a scrawny kid who had never seen men with large

muscles or who were in shape like the ones I saw in that magazine. *Huh, this is interesting,* I thought. *I want to work out and look like them, too.*

The only problem: I'd never worked out.

I knew nothing about how to build muscles or to get stronger. But like everything in my life, I figured, "Fuck it. I'll teach myself how to work out." I bought a membership to Bally Total Fitness, and for the first three to four months, I was the skinny kid too embarrassed to step into the free weight area. I didn't want to be the guy lifting twenty-five-pound weights when the other men were easily hoisting 175 pounds and more. I stuck to the machines, where I felt safe and comfortable.

Then I hit a breaking point. I wasn't making much progress. But I watched the men in the free weight area do great and thought, *I'll be damned if I'm not going to learn what they're doing.* I felt that fire in my gut to leave my comfort zone and to lift weights like them one day.

I gave myself a tough-love pep talk. *Guess what?* I said to myself. *I don't care what people think about me. I have a goal. I want to achieve my goal, and the only way I can do this is to break through and get into the weight room. I have to do whatever I have to do.*

I walked in, looked at the sixty-pound dumbbells, and set a goal. I said, *I'll lift those sixty- pound weights, but in the meantime, I will start light.* Every month, I bought *Flex* to learn new lifting techniques, different exercises, and about the key role diet plays in achieving my fitness goals. I started lifting lighter weights and bumped up my weight as I grew stronger.

I started out knowing nothing about weight lifting, but I was determined to learn. I learned so much and sculpted a good enough body that I became a personal trainer and helped other people realize their goals, too. Personal training became another avenue for me to earn cash. It meant sacrificing time on my weekends, but to me, it was more than a fair trade.

About four and a half years into my stint at Nationwide Insurance, one of my personal training clients suggested I go to work for his dad. "I've been to your house," I told him, "and it's massive. I have no idea what your dad does for work." Staying true to my roots, I told the guy his father could be a drug dealer for all I knew. I didn't really think he was, but then again, anything is possible given what I've seen.

My client laughed and assured me his dad wasn't a drug dealer.

I agreed to meet his father, Mr. Gentry. Turns out, he owned a consumer finance business. He built a fleet of companies that made money by making small loans—anywhere from $50 to $1,000—to people like the ones I knew in Dayton, people like my mom who struggled to keep up with the bills. He offered me low wages, something like $1,500 a month, much less than what I earned at the insurance company and working as a trainer.

But he roped me in when he said, "Hell, Joe-Van [he always pronounced my name in a thick, Texas drawl], you got more college than I do. I only have a high school diploma."

A high school degree, that's it? I thought. I was impressed. When I met him, he had more than four hundred branches of his company throughout the United States. How had one man built a massive company starting with just one and with only a high school degree? I wanted to learn from him.

I accepted the position and quickly put to work the lessons from Uncle Bobby, my mom, and my dad about hustling, grinding, and never stopping. I had gotten a taste of corporate America and started to learn the game at Nationwide; now I had the chance to put it all together to propel my career.

He had me start in what they called the proofing department. I sat in a windowless room waiting for the other consumer finance offices from around the country to send in their daily reports and deposit slips. Once a report came through, I went through one-by-one to check that every deposit matched the number in the computer.

By the six-month mark, I was restless and frustrated. It was tedious work, and this wasn't what I had joined the company for. I wanted to learn, I wanted to grow. I needed an angle, an opportunity to get out from where I was working. It was no different than life on the streets, trying to wrangle a free lunch from a little girl, studying hard so I could win that pair of Air Jordans that Uncle Bobby promised me, or even stealing Oreos so my kid sister could have a birthday. Everything on the streets is about finding an opening and taking advantage, turning three dollars into six dollars.

I asked the woman who oversaw the department what the record was for the most reports proofed in a day. She told me forty. That night, I drove home thinking about my next move. I decided that tomorrow, I would crush the record.

The next day, I proofed seventy-two documents. I drove home with a small smile for accomplishing my goal and thought about how I needed to up my game even more. I had to show them that my number wasn't a fluke.

The next day, I busted my record and tore through seventy-five documents. I did this day after day after day, never quitting, and outworking everyone next to me.

Eventually, my efforts and discipline paid off. Word made it all the way up the food chain to Mr. Gentry, who summoned me to his office. He stared at me from behind his giant desk, as if trying to discover my secret. I stood, silently, looking him in the eye, just as Uncle Bobby had taught me. Finally, he broke the silence.

"Obviously, you don't want to continue to do what you're doing," he said.

"No, sir," I responded, still using my Uncle Bobby manners.

"You have way more talent and drive than that. Hell, son, what do you want to do?" He asked with his head cocked to the side, still trying to figure me out.

Without missing a beat, I said, "I want to be in that picture, sir," and pointed to the picture on the wall behind him. "I want to be one of those folks." Those folks were the management team—the leaders, executive vice presidents, and partners at the company.

His eyes widened. "Hell, you're ambitious, aren't you, Joe-Van?"

I nodded. "You asked me what I wanted, sir, and that's what I want."

My third grade teacher, Ms. Dedak, used to tell me, "There are no stupid questions." I took that literally, and I believe that to this day. I'll ask for anything and everything that I want. If I'm getting on a plane, I'll ask for a free upgrade. You'd be surprised how many times they say yes, and it's all because I took the time to ask for what I wanted.

Even in the businesses I run today, I always ask for what I want. When I was the president of Headspring, a technology company, I remember I was about to get on a conference call with our chief architect and a *Fortune* 100 company that we were negotiating with. I told the chief architect that we were going to ask for $1 million for our product. He balked and tried to talk me out it, saying we'd scare them off if we threw out that number.

No, I told him, the worst that can happen is they tell us no. They want to do business with us. If they say no to our first offer, then we go down from there. We'd accept $350,000 for this engagement, but if they want to pay us more, then that's even better.

He was looking at it from the perspective of loss. I choose to think big. I choose to believe things can always get better for me. Thinking big, achieving your goals, and believing it can always get better means having to ask for what you want, without reservation or embarrassment. We closed that deal for $550,000, two hundred thousand more than we would've accepted.

I always tell the people I mentor to ask for more, to ask for what they want. Then, once they reach their goal, like making six figures, to think bigger, if they want. I've achieved success in life because I've never limited myself.

When I told Mr. Gentry what I wanted, he didn't say no, and he didn't tell me I couldn't achieve it. Instead, he said, "OK." And he gave me the chance to see what I could do with an opportunity.

He promoted me from proofing documents. My job now was to travel across the country and visit different offices and learn everything about how this business worked—what each branch did, why they did it, the consumer finance laws, and all the things that went into running one of his businesses.

For three months, I traveled for Mr. Gentry, putting my observational skills to work, listening, and learning the ins and outs of his business. My job was to sort out issues and to reconcile statements. I took the sliver of an opening and made sure to do my best with the responsibilities handed to me.

I remember in Shreveport, Louisiana, I would stay at the office until 11:00 p.m. sorting through the financial statements and the client backgrounds to make sense of what was going wrong and what was happening at the office. The normal workday was 8:00 a.m. to 5:00 p.m. But I put in the extra work and effort, knowing again, that my discipline and dedication would pay off.

Throughout my career, I've always put in the time, done the work, and behaved in a disciplined and diligent way. That's what it takes to succeed. That's what it takes to climb the ranks.

I once heard a wealthy gentleman say, "I work only half days. I just have to decide which twelve hours of the day I want to work." I laughed when I heard that quote, and I still laugh at it today. This is how I've lived. If I had to grind twelve hours to get the job done, then I did it. If I had to grind eighteen hours, then I did that, too. Whatever it takes to get what I want. I'll never stop until the job is done and I've achieved my goal.

Mr. Gentry never forced me to put in extra hours when I was on the road. I did it knowing that my work, effort, and results would make it back to him, which would create more opportunities for myself to advance in the company and professionally.

I was right, and it didn't take long for my hard work to pay off.

On a rare day at the home office, I heard a "Joe-Van" called. "Coming!" I called back, as though it was Uncle Bobby asking for me. "Yes, sir," I said as soon as I stood in front of Mr. Gentry.

"Hell, son, if I had eleven more of you, I could take over the world," he said to me.

His praise made me beam with pride. Even today, despite successes and accolades, this one small sentence remains one of the greatest compliments I've ever received.

In many ways, I was still a kid when Mr. Gentry called me into his office. I was twenty-three years old, and I had so much to learn about running a business and managing people. I had a lot of growing left to do, too, but in that moment, it was as though my hard work, discipline, hustle, and ability to grind paid off. Those late nights working until 11:00 p.m. made a difference. Setting the record for proofing statements had made a difference. I earned that compliment, just like I had earned that pair of Air Jordans from Uncle Bobby. And Mr. Gentry had praised me in front of all those vice presidents and district supervisors. What an accomplishment that was for me.

But Mr. Gentry wasn't done. He announced that he was promoting me to become a new area vice president and he was giving me my pick of locations. My choices were Shreveport, Louisiana; Las Vegas, Nevada; or Portland, Oregon.

I had traveled to Louisiana a lot for the company and figured he'd plunk me down there. That place was second only to Dayton to me in worst places to live. I had zero desire to be in Shreveport. Because I didn't drink or gamble, Vegas held no interest for me either. That left Portland, Oregon, which sounded interesting.

Mr. Gentry said he'd send me with his son, Cory, to Portland to look around and to see if I liked the area.

Cory and I flew to Portland, Oregon. As soon as I stepped off the plane, I made my choice. Portland, Oregon, was going to be my new home.

At twenty-three years old, I stood in the airport, looking around and feeling that I was ready to show the world what

I was made of. Mr. Gentry had cracked the door open for me when he gave me a job in the proofing department, but I busted through to blaze my own trail by working hard to create opportunity after opportunity to move up the ranks of his company. All because I used my discipline, hard work, hustle, grind, and manners. All because I did the work to earn it, then *asked* for what I wanted, without fear, and didn't rest until it was mine.

That's the thing that I believe I got right and that so many people in my position don't. Yeah, I didn't have many opportunities. A lot of people don't. However, the ONLY way forward was to work hard at the ones I had and then use those opportunities to get more. That's the only way out, the only path forward, to get from where I was to where I wanted to be. Hard work and hustle.

When I left for Portland, I was bound and determined to keep looking for ways to create more opportunities, each one bigger and better than the last.

EIGHT

Oregon

——

LOVE AT FIRST SIGHT. THAT'S HOW IT WAS FOR ME WHEN I stepped off the plane in Portland. It was everything that Dayton, Ohio, wasn't. I saw hills, mountains, and trees everywhere. And the air? Oh, it smelled fresh. I arrived in Portland in January, when most people find it at its bleakest, yet it was still magical in my eyes.

I found a place to live in an immaculately kept suburb of Portland called Lake Oswego. The guy at a local gas station suggested the place, saying that if you have money, "it's the best place to live in Portland."

Growing up in a segregated place like Dayton made me hyperaware of my surroundings. In San Antonio, I grew accustomed to living next to many men and women of

Hispanic descent. But I took one look around Lake Oswego and thought, *Ha! Not too many black people or people of color out here*. Shortly after I moved to Lake Oswego, I learned it had a nickname: Lake No Negro, the locals called it. Fitting.

Oregon was very much like Dayton at the time in regard to race—you were either black or white. Someone with my complexion screamed mixed race.

Although I'd found some success in business, I was still coming into my own, still learning how society worked, and still learning how your economic status shifted society's perception of you. The issue of race dominated national headlines around this time. The country was fresh off the Rodney King controversy and the O. J. Simpson trial.

One night, I was on my way home from the office, driving my Jeep Grand Cherokee, when I caught the flash of blue lights in my rearview mirror. A cop signaled for me to pull over.

The officer approached my window and asked to see my license. "What are you doing out here?" he asked.

"What do you mean *out here*?" I said, confused.

"Well, in Lake Oswego."

"Well, I live here."

"You sure about that?" he said condescendingly, as if he couldn't believe a person like me would live in Lake Oswego.

"Yeah," I said. "I live up the hill here."

The officer stared hard at me. "You live up the hill?" Again, he said it as though it was the most ludicrous thing he'd ever heard.

"Yeah," I replied, somewhat annoyed and confused as to why the officer was giving me a hard time.

As experienced as I was at certain things, I was still naïve at times. When I got home, I realized why I'd been pulled over. It wasn't because I broke any laws; he was profiling me. It was because of my skin color. I didn't look like I belonged in the community where I was living. The realization blew me away. I'd experienced racism before but never racial profiling.

Without understanding the weight of his actions, the officer placed a chip on my shoulder that day—a chip that drove me to show everyone that I was more than just my skin color. I'd always struggled to be accepted by people, but now, I saw firsthand how money could force people to accept me—whether they wanted to or not. When I was broke, people could (and did) say to me, "Nigger, go home," or, "Get the fuck out of here."

But now that I had money, there wasn't anything they could do about me. Behind my back, they could judge or talk about me, but to my face, they had to behave differently. Without money in my pocket, they could deny me entry into their gated communities. But with money, I had as much right to live in a community like Lake Oswego or join the fancy country club as anyone.

The officer also confirmed my theory that the people who control the money control the game. Not only that, money gave you power to *win* the game. Having money meant I could buy a washer and dryer instead of having to use the laundromat. Having money meant I could get a condo in a beautiful area instead of living in the hood. Having money meant I could buy a car to run errands instead of having to take the bus. Having money meant I could buy health insurance instead of having to rely on the system.

Having money changes *everything* about your life.

The officer's action validated my view of society and triggered the voice inside of me that said, "I'm going to work harder and smarter to earn more money, to claim my power, and to gain greater control over my life. And I won't stop until I get it."

Being racially profiled was a great gift. When the cop pulled me over, I realized he had nothing on me. He had nothing to hold over my head. I bought my Jeep Grand Cherokee and my condo in Lake Oswego with my money that I earned legally.

I was free, a feeling that pimps, drug dealers, and hustlers like my dad never know. When you lead a lifestyle like theirs, you're constantly looking over your shoulder in fear—fear that someone from the streets will overtake you, fear that you'll land in prison, or fear that you'll end up dead, riddled with bullets or stab wounds.

I didn't have to look over my shoulder like my dad. I had nothing to worry about when the cop pulled me over. I had made money. I had a career. I had a vice president title next to my name. I had a nice car. Nobody could touch me.

I was walking a different path than my father, and I was succeeding.

Who knew racial profiling would validate the life path I had chosen and created for myself?

SUCCESS IN OREGON

I went to Portland to manage three offices for Mr. Gentry. About a month into my new role, the phone rang. I picked up the receiver to the sound of, "Hello, Joe-Van. How's it going, son?"

"Mr. Gentry, it's going great!" I told him. "Thank you for this opportunity. I appreciate it, sir." I always made sure he knew how grateful I was. Even though I knew I created the opportunity for myself, I figured it was still wise to let the man signing my paycheck know that I appreciated the position.

"Great, great to hear, son. Here's what I want you to do now. I want you to go down to Eugene, Oregon, and open a new office. Are you OK with that?"

Without hesitating, I said, "Yes, sir."

"OK. Let me know what you need and keep me posted on how it goes."

"Yes, sir, I'm on it."

I hung up the phone and leaned back in my chair. *Holy shit,* I thought. *What am I supposed to do to open a new office?* Instead of panicking, I said to myself, *OK, JeVon, let's take a step back to think this through.* I had three offices I oversaw that all looked identical. I'd also seen many offices during my travels throughout the company, and they all looked the same, too. *OK, I can do this. I'll replicate the office exactly, layout for layout, as all the others.*

All right, I thought, *what's next? Well, first things first—I need to drive to Eugene to find space.*

When I got to Eugene, I drove around hunting for "For Rent" signs. I found nothing. Growing impatient, I pulled off to the side of the road to think my dilemma through. There has to be someone who can help me find a place, I presumed.

Sure enough, I found a commercial realtor to help. The agent showed me office space. Next, I pulled the leases for our three offices and gave them to the realtor, explaining I wanted the same deal. Before long, I had office space that needed filling, so I made a checklist of the office equipment. Then I purchased the same things we had in Portland, new or used, for the Eugene branch.

For weeks, I made the two- to two-and-a-half-hour drive back and forth between Portland and Eugene. When the day came to officially open the office, I took a picture of me, grinning, in front of the building.

It was a proud moment, one that I would experience again as I opened two more offices in Oregon for Mr. Gentry.

To me, failure was never an option. Mr. Gentry gave me a mission and I accepted it. From there, it was about working hard *and* smart to go from nothing to something.

People often say that, to succeed, you have to work smarter, not harder. That's bullshit. You have to do both.

In fact, you have to work harder at being smarter to succeed. The hot topic of finding a work-life balance is a myth. If you want to succeed at anything, you have to put in the work, and you have to put in the time. Yes, this requires sacrifice. It may mean giving up a vacation, time spent with family or friends, or pursuing a hobby. But that's what it takes to be great. I've never regretted the sacrifices I've made; all have been worth it.

* * *

I grew and learned incredible lessons from my experiences in Oregon, and most of it was because Mr. Gentry didn't train me. He didn't hand me a manual that explained how I was supposed to manage the offices or people. Each office had its own manager, all of them older than little twenty-three-year-old me. When the managers first met me, I swear their eyes screamed, "Who the hell are you?"

Basically, I was the business owner; I was the boss making all the day-to-day decisions. I handled bank deposits. I managed the teams. I interacted with clients. I cleaned up every problem and mess, both literal and figurative ones. Yes, when the office needed cleaning, I cleaned it. The only thing headquarters handled was payroll.

I learned everything on the fly, by watching and methodically thinking through each problem I encountered. I remember receiving a call from the police station at 2:30 a.m. early in my tenure as regional vice president. Someone had broken into our office, and I needed to go to the station to file a police report immediately. Because we were a consumer finance and loan business that made small loans—from $50 to $1,000—our offices were in shady parts of town. I got this call three times over a thirty-day period. No one told me how to handle it; I just figured it out and did it.

Then there was the time I got a call from one of the managers, a woman in her mid-to-late forties, in the middle of the night. Her fourteen-year-old daughter just died. What was I supposed to say to her? How was I supposed to respond? "You know, take care of your family," I told her. "Don't worry about the office. Be there for your family and call me if you need anything." I didn't know what else to say. There's no training manual for these types of situations.

Our policy said she got three days for bereavement. I read that and thought, *Hell no*. No way was I going to tell her she had to get back to work after suffering through that trauma. I made my own rules. She took ten days off before coming back to work. This event was a real-life lesson in empathy, sympathy, and how to deal with the people I managed and worked with.

My time in Oregon was filled with lessons like these that shaped and formed my perception of how to succeed in business and in managing people.

NEW OPPORTUNITIES

When I first arrived in Portland, Mr. Gentry told me the most important part of my job was to pass the state audits. "Yes, sir!" I replied enthusiastically. I knew my goal, and I was ready for the auditors.

The thing with auditors is they never tell you when they are coming; they just show up. So you have to always be ready. The first time an auditor appeared on my watch, I nervously waited as he went through our financials, tapping his calculator keys and flipping pages.

Finally, the verdict was in: I passed.

Eager to share the good news, I called Mr. Gentry. "Good job, Joe-Van," he said.

I set a goal, accomplished it, and smiled with pride as I stood on top of the world. Still, I wasn't completely satisfied. I learned that the highest score is an "exceptional." That's what I wanted. Just passing the audits wasn't good enough. I had to crush them. I had to be the best. To do this, I needed to learn the rules. I needed to understand what the auditors looked for.

Why not go directly to the source? I thought. So I called the auditor's office and asked how I could get an exceptional mark. The auditor kindly walked me through their expectations and laid out the rules.

The next time the office was audited, it received an exceptional ranking. Once you know the rules and expectations—whether that's for society-at-large, the company you're working for, or someone like the auditor—you know what you need to do to surpass them or mold them to your advantage.

Immediately, I dialed Mr. Gentry. "The auditors just left," I said.

"What happened?"

"We got an exceptional mark," I burst out.

"You're kidding me, Joe-Van," Mr. Gentry said, surprise evident in his tone.

"No, sir."

"Well, that's just great. Great job, Joe-Van, great job!"

Telling Mr. Gentry about the exceptional rating was like showing Uncle Bobby my report card with Bs and Cs. Mr. Gentry had become like a father figure to me, and hearing his praise made me feel proud, like I had accomplished something big. He sent me a little extra in my check after the auditor's rating as a little thank you and acknowledgment for a job well done.

* * *

One of the best parts of my job in Portland was that I got a master class in the inner workings of a business—and I discovered I loved it! I loved crunching the numbers and looking at profits and losses. I loved learning about compound interest. I loved making money.

As much as I loved it, I also realized we were basically running a hustle, almost like a drug deal, except legal.

Our business was payday loans. We would loan small

amounts of money, from $50 to $1,000. How it worked was, say we loaned someone $400. The person would be responsible for seven monthly payments of $92.28. That means, on a $400 loan, he or she would have to pay back $646.02.

And then we'd make even more money by renewing lendees. When they came in the last time, we'd tell them to keep that last payment, and we'd refinance the loan, which would start over in thirty days. Or we'd get them to take more money.

I understood my role in the company, the rules of this game, and how to ensure the company remained profitable. My mastery of the game was evident in the figures for the companies under my watch. The percentages, the profit we made, went through the roof. My base office in Portland had never turned a profit in its two and a half years of existence. Once under my control, profits rained down.

Once I locked in the refinancing game, I looked deeper into the numbers and learned a shocking fact: in Oregon, you can garnish wages for anything. In many states, like Texas, only taxes and child support can be withheld. But in Oregon, if someone didn't pay us, then I could file a small claims lawsuit against him or her that would cost me $50. The court would award me what the borrower owed

($646.02) plus an additional $150. Each month, Oregon would withhold a part of this person's paychecks and would give the wages to me until the debts were paid off.

I couldn't believe it. If someone didn't pay my company, all I had to do was take them to small claims court, and his or her wages would be garnished, and I'd get *extra* money.

I acted immediately. I had put our books in order, so I knew exactly who was late in making payments. I immediately started filing lawsuit after lawsuit in small claims court against them.

Angry men and women flooded the office demanding to know why I had money taken out of their checks. I calmly explained the situation and asked them how they wanted to work things out. Most of the time, people calmed down, although many times, the conversations became heated. I used my skills at talking to people, which I'd learned by watching my father talk to everyone, to smooth over and deescalate most situations. In the end, most people paid their bills, and we turned an extra profit.

It wasn't long before I learned something else groundbreaking: many of our clients borrowed money from our two competitors to pay our loans or vice versa. I assumed the same people who weren't making their payments on the loans I gave them likely had outstanding loans with our competitors, too. I called the managers at our competitors' offices, befriended them, and then politely asked if we shared clients. It turned out that about 50 percent of our client base was the same.

But unlike my company, none of my competitors were suing and garnishing wages from our shared clients.

I saw a profit gold mine in front of me. If we bought those companies, we could sue the clients for their outstanding bills, make the money we loaned back, and earn additional profit. I developed a thorough proposal to buy out our two competitors and presented it to Mr. Gentry. He immediately agreed.

We snatched up our competitors, and as I predicted, we turned a profit with my strategy. All because I learned the rules in Oregon.

When I moved to Portland, Mr. Gentry owned three offices. When I left, three years later, we were eight strong.

* * *

Oregon held many big moments and lessons for me. One of the biggest shifts in my career came when headquarters ordered me letterhead that read "J. McCormick."

It looked pretty cool to me. Seeing my name that way also got my wheels spinning. I thought about how quick people, like the police officer, were to pass judgment on me because of my skin. I thought about how Mr. Gentry called me "Joe-Van." It was like I grabbed all these different pieces and started putting together a jigsaw puzzle.

The finished picture confirmed what I knew: people would stereotype me based on my skin and my name, JeVon.

I couldn't do anything about the color of my skin, but seeing J. McCormick on paper was a revelation. Who could stereotype me based on an initial? No one. And you couldn't pass judgment based on my last name, which happens to be Irish.

This was the moment when I decided to drop going by my given name, JeVon, and started going by my initials. I didn't like just the *J*—that was boring to me—so I took my middle name, Thomas, to create *JT McCormick*.

It was genius. If someone saw JT on a piece of paper, they couldn't tell I was of mixed race. Then I thought about the president of Nationwide Insurance, how he was a black man who spoke eloquently and articulately. *If I was changing my name, I mused, I bet I could change my dialect. I could perfect it, so that when I'm on the phone with people, they won't know my race by the sound of my voice.*

The final act was for me to polish my presentation skills to help me avoid being immediately labeled. I never wanted someone to turn down a phone call or avoid a conversation with me because of an inaccurate judgment made based on my skin color.

I'd spent my entire life being judged by everyone because of my race. I wanted a fresh start. I wanted a chance to rise and be seen for my work ethic, grind, hustle, and commitment.

I didn't create society, but I was learning how to play its game. I was learning the rules for how the world worked so I could make society and its rules work in my favor. I was tailoring myself, molding who I was to become what society demanded I become in order to succeed. If that meant taking my name, JeVon Thomas McCormick, and switching it to JT McCormick, then so be it. I'd do it, and I'd do it proudly if it meant people would see beyond my skin and name.

And they have. As I got older and made sales calls, I blended in. No one knew I was of mixed race. No one could tell I was raised on the streets of Dayton.

Martin Luther King Jr.'s "I Have a Dream" speech has always gripped me. I've wanted what Dr. King spoke about: to be judged on the content of my character rather than the color of my skin.

Even today, with all my successes, I still don't want anyone to look at my race and judge me. I don't want people stereotyping me because my father was a drug-dealing pimp and my mom grew up in an orphanage and we were poor. I don't want people to assume anything about me because I lack the academic credentials or an MBA. I want to be judged on my work ethic, on my ability to get the job done and to achieve results. That's it.

Well, sometimes you have to help people judge you based on your character alone. And the way you present yourself is a huge part of helping them.

AN EMOTIONAL DECISION

I heard the front office door open behind me. I turned and everything froze. A white lady with long dark hair and a little boy with light brown skin and curly hair stood in front of me.

Mixed-race people know other mixed-race people, especially in Oregon where you were either white or black. Gazing at the woman and her son was like looking at a picture of me and my mom. I asked her, immediately, "Is your son mixed—half white, half black?"

She said, "Yes."

I knew it as soon as I saw him.

She had come to make a payment on her bill. I nodded and proceeded to catalog her information. She handed me her money and I looked at her bill. My world tilted.

She was making a payment, a late one at that, on a *$100 loan*.

My throat closed a little as I choked down my emotions. This was me and my mom. This was a woman killing herself to support her son, with no father, and she had to take out payday loans. It all came back to me in a flash. The pain, the hunger, the fear, and the uncertainty.

The woman handed me her money, thanked me quietly, and then walked out, hand in hand with her son. I followed them to the door, stopping in front of the glass. Through the window, I watched them walk to the bus stop.

I couldn't witness the scene any longer. My eyes burned as I quickly turned away from the door and rushed to the backroom. I dropped onto a metal chair and put my head into my hands.

I sobbed. I felt awful. I felt awful for the lady struggling to get by, for her son, for what we were doing to them, and for the entire situation.

When I emerged from the backroom, my staff asked why I didn't try to renew her, try to get her to refinance her loan so we could make more money. That's what we always did, right?

As soon as I looked at her and her son, I had no intention of renewing her. Until that day, I never thought hard or looked closely at our business and what we did.

But in that moment, when I stared into her eyes, I saw the role a business like ours played in keeping people like her stuck in a perpetual system of poverty. If you have to borrow $100, such a small sum (but huge for many people), how does someone ever get out of that vicious cycle?

That one encounter tore me apart. I flashed back to my mom and I with nothing to eat for dinner, trudging through the snow with bread bags on our feet, waiting in the rain for the bus with our dirty clothes loaded in black Hefty lawn bags.

I tried to shake the experience off, but I couldn't. I couldn't get past the role I was playing in these people's lives. Like I said, this was a hustle. A legal hustle, but it was still a hustle. Once confronted with the facts of my role, I could no longer do it. I could not be part of something that hustled women like my mother. It wasn't right.

It couldn't have been more than three weeks later when I called Mr. Gentry to tell him I was done.

"Whoa, Joe-Van, what's the problem?" he said, concern lacing his voice.

"I want to move on, sir. I got other things," I said.

"What are you moving on to?"

"I don't know, but I don't want to do this anymore."

My feelings are mixed when it comes to these sorts of businesses. There are always two sides. No one forces anyone to borrow money, and it is legal. Up until that moment with the woman and her son, I had ignored my emotions. I took the attitude of my father, who loved to remind me that the only difference between the drug dealer and the CEO of Budweiser was man made one vice illegal, the other legal.

That's the lens through which I viewed the consumer finance industry. Society made it legal, and I didn't force anyone to take a loan; I simply played by the rules as they were written.

But seeing that woman and her child, a mirror image of me and my mom, brought all my buried emotions to the surface. I couldn't separate what we were doing from the impact it had on people's lives anymore. Because I *knew*. I knew what it was like to walk in their shoes.

That was the moment when it struck me: *just because society has made something legal doesn't make it right.*

This isn't a critique on Mr. Gentry or companies like his. I still send him a Christmas card each holiday season, and he remains one of the most influential figures in my life, right next to my mom and Uncle Bobby.

However, I reached the point in my career where I couldn't look the other way. I may have been making my money legally, unlike my dad, but it didn't feel good. It didn't feel right to me. I was still exploiting people. I might as well have been a criminal.

I needed to get out, and fortunately for me, I had money in savings and had made some wise investments that afforded me the chance to leave my job and start fresh.

Starting fresh meant returning to Texas, to San Antonio and my mom, who was married by now. She helped me find a rental house, so when I arrived in the city, I was ready to hit the pavement in search of my next stepping stone.

NINE

The Mortgage Industry

―――

BY NOW, I WAS TWENTY-SIX, AND AFTER MY SUCCESS building Mr. Gentry's consumer finance businesses in Portland, I believed I could do anything I wanted. Nothing would stand in my way.

Now the question I needed to answer was, what did I want to do next?

I'd fallen in love with finance, money, and business. I loved how dollars made everything work, and how the person with the money controlled the game.

So I grabbed the local newspaper (because this was pre-internet) and saw an ad for a company hiring a mortgage processor. I wasn't familiar with the mortgage industry. I read a little about it and was intrigued. This was the business tied to the biggest purchase that most people make in their lifetimes: their homes. And the way the money moved in the transaction was interesting. I could learn a lot in that industry.

I sent résumés out (for JT McCormick) to several mortgage companies. But I didn't stop with one outreach. I followed up in person with each company I sent my résumé to.

I did this because I learned that most people would submit a résumé and that's it. They'd wait for a callback. Few people took the initiative. I wanted to stand out, so I kept following up. I'd show up at the office, explaining that I had submitted my résumé and would appreciate the opportunity to speak with the hiring manager or the person doing the hiring. Or I'd call and ask how things were going. I was always polite but always persistent.

This tactic was inspired by a few stories I'd read shortly after I returned home to San Antonio. One story that stuck with me was by Napoleon Hill in his book *Think and Grow Rich*. The story was about a person who was trying to get a job with a company. At first, he reached out to the company once a month. Then, he reached out once a week, once a day, and finally hourly until the company hired him.

Another story that left an impression was about Thomas Edison and the lightbulb. He supposedly failed ten thousand times before succeeding. I say you only fail if you stop trying. If you keep going, you don't fail. You just reset, reassess what you need to do, make adjustments, and then continue to move closer to your goal. Edison didn't fail ten thousand times; it just took him ten thousand attempts to learn the way to do it right.

All these tiny lessons about persistence, I took to heart. If these individuals could succeed simply by their sheer will to never give up, then so could I. For me, if you just work on following up, being persistent, consistent, and polite, you can get ahead of most people in our society. Most people quickly give up.

Plus, follow up was easy to me. If I had to call ten people to follow up on the résumés I submitted, then I was going to do it because making phone calls was *nothing* compared to what I endured as a kid. My childhood was hard. Making phone calls wasn't. Rejection never bothered me.

I remember thinking a lot about my mom during this period of my life as I tried to find a job in the mortgage industry.

Mom always did what she had to do to get by. I'm sure there were times my mom wanted to quit. I'm sure there were moments she had to wonder why she had to have me in the first place. Despite how difficult her life was, she never gave up. She never quit; she always kept going. That memory inspired me to keep pursuing the mortgage companies, to make one more phone call, to stop by one more office until I found my job. Mom did what she had to do to just survive. I would do what I needed to in order to succeed.

Eventually, my efforts paid off, and a lady who owned a small mom-and-pop mortgage company brought me in for an interview.

"What do you know about mortgages?" she asked.

"Nothing," I said. "But I can tell you that no one in your company will outwork me."

She looked at my background and what I'd accomplished with Mr. Gentry over the last three years. It was enough to convince her to give me a shot. She offered me a position, and this became my introduction to the world of mortgage lending. I learned how to process loans and then how to be a loan officer under her tutelage.

*　*　*

One of the people who used to come into the mom-and-pop mortgage office was a Countrywide Home Loans account executive. Before the credit crisis of 2009, Countrywide was one of the biggest lenders for mortgages in the world. I was intrigued by this account executive. All she did was come to our office, talk to the loan officers, and ask if we had any loans we wanted her to look at. She was looking to purchase our loans. Some days, she would bring cookies, and she would make it a point to talk to everybody she greeted. I watched her and thought to myself, *Hey, I'm good at talking to people like her.* She reminded me a little of my father and how he could talk to anyone and make them feel like they were his friend.

One day, I asked her about her job and what it entailed. She gave me the rundown and mentioned they had an opening for another account executive. I applied, and Countrywide hired me to go from one small mom-and-pop mortgage company to another, like the one I previously worked at, to sell our services. My job was to get them to give us their loans in exchange for a good rate.

Like everywhere else in life, I paid attention to the people and the money, and I realized that the people I needed to connect with weren't loan officers—the ones working with homeowners—but rather, the loan processors.

I made it my mission to befriend the loan processors, the

ones most of my colleagues ignored. Other account executives thought the real power was with the loan officers. They were the six-figure earners, after all. The loan processors were behind the scenes, shuffling papers, and pooling loans. However, they were the real power brokers. They were the ones determining which company to sell their loans to, loans that my company wanted to purchase.

At Countrywide, I was given what the company called a marketing budget. Basically, they gave me money every month to wine and dine people. This still blows my mind! Growing up, we didn't have a spare dime for a chocolate milk, and no one gave us any spare change, but here people were literally throwing money at me, telling me to go feed and take care of people.

Most of the loan processors were female, so thinking creatively, I used the money Countrywide gave to me to wine and dine people to send every female loan processor in my service area a dozen roses. This resulted in a flood of business for me.

Then, taking a page out of the days proofing for Mr. Gentry, I asked my Countrywide branch manager what the record was for the most loans brought in over one day. He said five, maybe six. I knew my goal.

The next day, I slapped ten loans onto the branch manager's desk.

"Are these ten loans from one place?" he asked, somewhat startled.

"No, ten different places."

"Damn, that's impressive."

In every position I've held, I've always looked for those advantages, the small slivers or cracks that I could use to create opportunities for myself to stand out from the crowd. Being average or just getting by never suited me. I'm competitive. I couldn't tell you where that comes from, but I've always wanted to be the best—that's always been my goal. And I've never stopped aspiring for more.

Once I knew the daily loan record at Countrywide, I aimed for the weekly, then the monthly, and then the yearly. I became the best account executive at Countrywide. I broke and set new records, and I did it because I understood one of the fundamental truths in business: if you build a solid relationship with someone, you can pretty much do any business you want with them.

* * *

My philosophy on treating people nicely came from two places: (1) my father, who instilled that lesson in me when I was a boy, and (2) my experiences in the insurance and mortgage industries. Those industries were the opposite of nice.

Most people in the insurance and mortgage industries were out for themselves, and that meant most were only out to make money. Profit is great, especially if you're a publicly traded company, because you have quarterly earnings to meet and shareholders to appease. But these two industries were different than most. They were ruthlessly selfish.

I learned the business from different angles, but it was all the same: everyone was focused on their personal gains. I ended up operating this way as well, in many ways. The mortgage industry was about answering the questions, "How do I serve *myself*?" "How do *I* get paid?" "How do *I* utilize (a nice way of saying "use") others to help me achieve what I'm after?"

Most people, including me, were out to make as much money as they could. They were out to advance their careers and their bank accounts, so they used any and all tools available to them to achieve their goals. I looked at the playing field before me and said, "What can I do for these people (like the loan processors) that in turn they can do for me?"

The difference between the mortgage industry and the consumer finance industry I was in previously was simple: I could convince myself that the mortgage industry was moral. I was helping people get houses, after all. I could not convince myself I was helping people by giving them $100 loans with high rates of interest.

Also, the mortgage industry allowed me to build relationships. I realized how treating people nicely, especially those in positions perceived as unimportant, could rake in more cash.

Yes, I knew that treating people nicely was important, and I would have treated them with respect and kindness anyway, but this was the first time I witnessed real, added benefit to my life from treating people well.

I built strong relationships because it helped me meet my goals. When I treated receptionists and executive assistants well, they were more willing to let me through to talk to their bosses.

I took the time to develop key relationships with the right people. I took the loan processors to lunch. I discovered who was married, their anniversary dates, and who had kids. Then I'd acknowledge those dates. I'd send catered lunches to their offices. Instead of approaching these women like most of the account executives who gave presentations on mortgage percentage points and the rate they'd give them, I focused on building meaningful relationships. People want to work with people they know and trust, so I started there.

Building strong relationships hinges on treating people the right way, on treating them nicely. It's easy to barrel over people when you're overcoming obstacles and traumatic events in your life, possibly using your past as motivation. I did that for a time.

But it would be a grave mistake to ignore people you think are below you. Every industry, every business has stand-ins for loan officers, the ones bringing in big dollars, and the loan processors are the ones behind the scenes wielding more influence.

I see *everyone*, and I treat *everyone*—especially those in the service industry, such as custodians, janitors, waiters, and administrative support—with respect. Actually, I probably treat those people better than I do the CEOs and others in the rich-and-famous category. Those high-ranking men and women have enough people kissing up to them.

I remember my days cleaning toilets, busing tables, and living in a class of people who are often ignored. That's partly why I go out of my way to acknowledge them, to show them respect and kindness. I remember being that person. Everyone deserves respect. And it helps you succeed. I will always support someone pursuing their dreams, working hard, and doing whatever it takes to succeed.

It takes twenty to thirty seconds to have an impact on someone's life. I prefer to take time to say, "Thank you," and to ask people, regardless of their position, how their day is going; to ask them, genuinely, "How are you doing?"; to say, "Have a good day!"; to say, "I appreciate your efforts"; or to look at their name tag and greet them by name. I'll even take a moment to send a letter to someone's boss in praise for an exceptional job.

When I take my wife on a date to the movies, I say hello to the person collecting our tickets. I'll look at their name tag, and say, "Hi, Steve. How's it going today?" Instantly, the person perks up, which gives me the next opening to ask if the movie is any good. I'll ask if he has seen it and whether he would recommend it. Immediately, the person is engaged in the conversation with me, and he wants to talk with me.

My dad was right (not in how he taught me the lesson, though): *you speak to everyone, you show respect to everyone, and you be nice to everyone.* This is a formula for success, whether you're a hustler on the streets or working your way through corporate America.

LEAVING THE GAME

After I was at Countrywide for about two years and doing very well, I met a man who was running a very profitable and complicated mortgage business. I met him because I went into his office trying to figure out if he had any loans that he would send over to Countrywide. He was impressed with my sales pitch and said, "Hey, you know what? I got something better for you. Why don't you come work for me?"

He sat me down, explained how his game of mortgages worked (how they're bought and sold and resold on Wall Street as investment vehicles), and told me I could join him. I was pretty much sold, but when he offered me a $15,000 signing bonus, I was 100 percent in.

I went to work for him, and my job was to find and buy the mortgages, exactly what I was doing with Countrywide. And I was damn good at it. In two years working for him, I probably made more than $500,000 in commissions.

The problem? What he was doing was highly illegal.

The whole explanation of his scheme is too long and complex for this book, but it basically boiled down to a Ponzi scheme. He would take people's money and then use it to get loans, which he would sell to Wall Street. It didn't look like anything illegal at all because everything was done through legit banks. And everyone who ever asked for their money back got it. He always paid up. Everything seemed legal to me.

I spent all my time hustling loans, just like at Countrywide, and didn't fully understand what we were doing on the other side. Thank God I had no idea, because the Securities and Exchange Commission (SEC) ended up raiding our office. I was completely cleared by the SEC. I was never charged with anything because I did nothing wrong. However, the man I worked for went to prison. In fact, he's still in prison now.

I avoided prison, but I still suffered. I lost everything.

Up to that point in my life, I had saved a decent amount of money, but I had all of my money invested in the company. I saw the returns coming in and going out; I thought it was a great deal, so I invested, too. And because it was essentially a pyramid scheme, I ended up losing it all.

Not only did I lose all of my invested money, but I also had no other money. I had made close to $1 million over the last seven years, and I blew it all.

I spent my money almost as fast as it came in, and all on

stupid stuff: trips to Vegas, gifts for friends, expensive cars. All that dumb shit that rappers and athletes buy before they go broke, I bought. And then I lost it.

It was so bad for me that I had to go to my best friend, Bishop, and my stepfather, EJ, and borrow money from them to pay my rent and bills.

That was one of the most humiliating times of my life. In some ways, it may have been worse than being poor as a kid. When I was a kid, I didn't know any different. I'd never made money.

But as an adult, I'd made a bunch of money. I thought I was out. I'd taken my friends and family to expensive dinners. I had shown off my expensive clothes, my fancy house, and my nice car. And now here I was, broke again, coming back asking for help.

The one difference was that now I had a marketable skill. I could sell. And if you can sell, you can always make more money.

I went back to straight mortgages. I got a job with Wachovia Bank, doing exactly what I'd been doing at Countrywide. This time, I doubled my hustle. I worked even harder than I had before. I was relentless.

Within a few months, I paid back my friends and family. Within two years, I became the Wachovia Mortgage banking lead in Texas.

This time, I also learned my lesson about money and spending. I sold almost everything I had (except my nice clothes), moved into a nice but small apartment, bought a reliable but inexpensive car, and saved as much money as I could.

In fact, I even went further than that. For five years, I bought almost nothing new—no new underwear, no new socks. Every dime that I made, I poured into the stock market.

And I spent all my spare time reading—not just casual reading. I lost all my money because I didn't know how to invest, or diversify, or understand anything about taxes, wealth management, or blind trusts. I lost hundreds of thousands of dollars because I didn't have enough information, because I hadn't done the work to understand what I was doing. I vowed to never make that mistake again.

I set about learning everything I could. I read every investing book, every magazine, every trade journal. I worked for Wachovia for a little more than four years and spent more time studying investing, the stock market, and financial planning on my own than most people who do it for a living.

I don't have much to say about this period of my life. Compared to my earlier years, it was pretty boring. Gym, work, read, sleep—that's all I did. But it was exciting to me. I felt like I was gaining more power every day. As I read more and learned more, I felt like I was seeing behind the curtain.

It's easy to learn the rules of Monopoly, but learning the real rules of money takes a lot longer. But once you do, it's exhilarating.

Then the mortgage crisis hit. In 2009, the mortgage industry collapsed under its own weight. Wachovia went under, was absorbed into another bank, and the mortgage division was shut down.

I was out of a job, except this time, I was in a much better position.

I came home from my last day at Wachovia and looked at my brokerage account. I was sitting on just under $1 million—cash. I'd had a good five-year run, both selling mortgages and playing the stock market. I'd learned from my mistakes.

* * *

Shortly after the banks collapsed and the economy tanked, my mom called wanting to know if I was part of the mess.

Admittedly, I took part in the reckless behavior that led to the crisis. I traded mortgage-backed securities on Wall Street and got rich off writing bad loans.

Many people working in the mortgage industry were guilty of writing loans for people who had no business buying homes. Of course, there were a few honest, upstanding mortgage brokers who operated with integrity. I don't want to make it sound like every single man or woman in the industry was flawed. However, the overwhelming majority of the people I came into contact with knowingly gave mortgages to homeowners who didn't have the money to afford their loans. Those mortgage brokers saw an opportunity to make money, so they funneled potential homeowners into borrowing whether it was the right choice for those individuals or not.

Now, the banks and mortgage brokers aren't solely to blame for the fiasco. Yes, they had a large role, but no one forced people to sign on the dotted line. No one told someone to go to Chase, Wells Fargo, or Wachovia to buy a home. Many people who took out the loans didn't take the time to properly research or understand what they were getting into. They didn't read through the contract, otherwise they would have realized that in two years, they had to refinance. If they failed to refinance, then the interest rate would spike from 5 percent to 9 percent, making the loan unaffordable for them.

It frustrated me then, and it still does now, that people didn't take thirty minutes to look through the contract and ask questions about their loan to fully understand what they were getting into. It's one thing to become upside down on a car loan, but it's another on a home.

I guess I can't judge that much, though, because I made a similar mistake in how I invested my money the first time around.

I knew the system was broken. Once I got to Wachovia, when I sold loans directly to homeowners, I created a document that outlined what people needed to know. Few loan officers did this, and many times, the future homeowner didn't care. They were focused on the loan amount and the rate. At Wachovia, we had something called a pick-a-pay loan. Customers could choose from four options. What does the average American choose for a payment option? The lowest monthly payment.

It pained me to watch this happen because it reminded me of the consumer finance industry. Just as I watched scores of people flow through Mr. Gentry's office become trapped, I saw the same thing happen in the mortgage industry. Lots of people jumped on cheap and easy money, and no one thought to ask what would happen when the bill came due.

The banks were wrong, and they don't deserve a free pass.

But each of us also has to take responsibility for our lives and all the decisions we make.

*　*　*

I have to be honest: had the credit crisis not happened, I probably would have stayed in the industry. The game and the cash hooked me. The lifestyle was great. And once I figured out the system, I quickly stacked my chips. Like I said, when the 2009 crisis hit, I was sitting on almost $1 million in cash. And this time, it wasn't in mortgages, so it was safe.

After Wachovia went under, with that kind of money, I was in no rush to move on. I didn't work for six months. I had my little six-hundred-square-foot apartment, I had one car, I had almost no expenses; life was nice. I went to the gym twice a day and had even more time to read. I wasn't blowing money; I was watching my money grow. If you didn't know me, you didn't know I had any money. In fact, even those closest to me didn't know.

I was alone, without a job, and single. It was the perfect opportunity for me to ask what I wanted in my life, and how I wanted to move forward. What was next for me? Who do I want to be as a person? What did I want to do for work? These were questions I had never asked myself.

I spent a considerable amount of time reflecting on my life, on how I got to where I was in that particular moment, and how I became the person I was. I looked back on the different events of my childhood and my adult life. I thought about how I got to Austin. I thought about my time with Mr. Gentry and what I did for that company. I thought about how my life would have been different if I had chosen Shreveport, Louisiana, instead of Portland, Oregon. I thought about how different my life was in Austin compared to my childhood in Dayton and my teenage years in San Antonio.

I'm a huge believer in reflecting on life and how I've lived it. There's a power in reflecting on achievements, what I did to create them, and also what I can do the next time to make it better. I'm a student of life. I'm constantly learning by reading and observing others, then testing and adapting my actions and behaviors to achieve my goals.

The one thing I didn't do as I sat around and reflected is regret. I don't regret anything about my past, nor would I change anything about it. Would I change it so my mom or my kid brother and sisters could have had better, easier lives? Absolutely, that I would change if I could. But for me? No, I wouldn't change anything because every single experience—the beatings, stints in juvenile detention, cleaning toilets, working in the insurance and mortgage industries, the horrific behavior and choices I made with the women I dated, all the pain and hurt I've endured and caused—has made me the man I am today.

I'm living and leading a life that I love, that I've achieved and created, because of my past.

We all make poor decisions in life; everyone does. We all go through tough experiences and our own traumatic events. I believe people can overcome them if they want to. They can make better decisions and amends for poor ones.

Everything is about the choices we make in life. If you make a bad decision, if you do something wrong, then what will you do from there? I struggled with decisions I made, and during my time of self-reflection after I left Wachovia, I saw this clearly. I didn't choose to be there at my dad's girlfriend's house. I didn't choose to be left alone to care for my brothers and sisters. I didn't choose to take those beatings, but I did choose to overcome them and become successful.

You have control over the choices you make in life, too, regardless of the experiences you have had. I made horrible choices in my life. Yes, it's true I never had proper role models. I never saw what a healthy relationship looked like.

But it was up to me to change that. I had to learn for myself.

I could have gone down the path of bad relationships that never lasted. But I sat back and realized it wasn't right; how I treated those women wasn't right. I realized I didn't want to be anything like my dad.

I chose to work on myself.

Today, my story about how I treat people has changed. I have a beautiful wife and children whom I love, protect, and care for deeply. Even my mom, when she visits me from her home in Wisconsin, says I'm a different person. I am. Like everything else in my life, I had to learn—by teaching myself, by observing, and by wanting to change—how to act in a relationship. I had to learn how to treat women, how to respect them, and how to conduct myself.

And I did it.

* * *

It was Christmas Eve, and I was alone. I went to Jack in a Box, loaded up on food, and came back to my apartment. I turned on *It's a Wonderful Life*, and maybe for the first time in my life, I was completely at peace. I woke on Christmas morning with nowhere to go, yet I was at peace.

It's hard to describe how I felt at this moment in my life. The word that comes to mind is *safe*, which was an unusual feeling for me. I didn't really know how to process it. It was like being on a different planet.

As safe and at peace as I felt, I also knew my life had to change. You can only go to the gym twice a day for so long, and you can only read so much. Money fixes a lot, but it can't fix your emotions, and it can't heal you. Money doesn't get you the thing that matters most in life: great relationships with people who love you.

I had crossed one finish line in my life; I had gotten to where I wanted to go in life—financially secure, safe, and at peace. But I had no idea what to do next, so I did the only thing I've always done in life. I kept moving.

TEN

Headspring

ON A COLD DAY IN FEBRUARY, MY PHONE RANG. IT WAS a recruiter calling to ask me if I was interested in working for a company called Insperity.

To this day, I have no idea how the recruiter found me. The recruiter explained that Insperity provided outsourced human resources (HR) services, such as payroll management, workers' compensation, healthcare insurances, and other employee benefits for companies. It essentially manages a company's entire human resources department.

I was intrigued. While working for Mr. Gentry, I developed my passion for business. And since then, I'd learned about almost every different facet of running a business: from selling, to reading balance sheets, to income statements, to operations. The things I didn't know about were employee benefits, workers' compensation, or anything about human resources.

I was still reading business books and going to the gym twice a day. My itch to keep moving needed to get scratched. I decided this was the perfect opportunity.

I worked at Insperity for two and a half years. It was like I had discovered the last piece of a jigsaw puzzle. Insperity had me doing what I was good at—building relationships with potential clients, selling services to companies, and negotiating deals. I learned all about employee benefits and the significant impact those have on a company.

During this time, I kept devouring business books, studying, and learning about leadership, investing, and decision making. I wanted to understand why leaders made certain decisions or passed up opportunities, or why they failed to see what was around the corner. I studied why Blockbuster passed up the opportunity to buy Netflix. I wanted to know why it took McDonald's ages to start serving breakfast 24/7. I had to know why BlackBerry didn't realize that the iPhone and Android were on its heels about to pry the industry from its grip.

Insperity was a great place for me to learn more about how

companies actually operated and created their strategies. I had to study what they needed to succeed in real, tangible ways, because it was my job to actually dig into the details and see the operations from the inside. I was able to get access to the deepest, most inner workings of dozens of *Fortune* 500 companies, because HR is the fuel that drives them. I saw inside the machine, and it was fascinating.

I'm still fascinated by the fact that anyone can learn anything he or she wants about publicly traded companies. All the information is available for anyone with the interest, desire, and willingness to look closer.

While at Insperity, I spent more than a year courting and trying to sell our services to Dustin, the owner of a software company called Headspring. Whereas other salespeople would likely have given up on the company, I stuck with my mother's never-give-up, never-quit, just-don't-stop, persistent attitude. That persistence paid off when I finally brought Headspring on board as a client, seventeen months after my first contact.

A month after closing our deal, my phone rang. This time, Dustin called me with an offer. He wanted me to work for him.

I just want to point something out: every job I ever got was because of my persistence and my work ethic. I showed the people who hired me what I would be like as a worker *before* they took me on. That lesson—show what you can do—is one that has served me my whole life.

Back to Headspring. I had no clue about software or the software industry. To me, that was a young person's game, and I was already thirty-eight—too old in my mind for what he wanted me to do. He disagreed. He said he could teach me about software; that was the easy part. What he wanted was my knowledge on how to sell, how to interact with people, and how to follow up. He needed me to build his sales department.

I didn't know about software, but I did know how to sell, how to interact with people, and how to follow up. That's the thing about selling and hustling—it's a skill that's transferrable to any company or market because ultimately, great salespeople are not selling products; they are building relationships. And I knew how to do that.

I agreed and joined the company as employee number thirteen. When I signed on, it was an enterprise software company that wrote software systems. One of the systems it wrote was for a state's juvenile case management. The software Headspring wrote tracked files for every youngster who went in and out of the juvenile detention system.

It seemed that no matter what job I had—working with Mr. Gentry, the mortgage industry, and then Headspring—my past was always just over my shoulder. No matter how much I ran from it, no matter how far I got, there it was, right behind me.

I was hired as the lowest-paid person in the company, which was fine with me. I had a lot of money in my bank account. I wasn't doing this just for the money. I realized an opportunity existed to help the company expand by creating and growing a sales team, which was something I had never done. Most of the talent in the organization were software engineers, and Dustin was right: no one knew how to sell, build relationships, and follow up like me. This was like working for Mr. Gentry all over again. Dustin was going to leave me alone to figure things out on my own. He cracked open a door for me, and I was going to bust through and see how far I could go.

I went from the lowest-paid person in the company all the way to president of the company in just two and a half years.

But before I could become president, I had to learn what it meant to be on a team, to be a team player, and the critical role that culture plays in the success of an organization.

CULTURE IS KEY

Headspring was the perfect place for me to showcase all the talents, mindsets, and behaviors I'd developed over the last three decades. However, there was also a lot of room to grow and ways for me to mature.

When I first arrived at Headspring, I was the business development guy. My goal: to grow the company. For a year, I crushed it. I brought in new business so rapidly that we had to move to a larger office to accommodate the new hires we had to bring in to keep pace with my new accounts. When we got to the new offices, someone jokingly called the space the "house that JT built."

I kept the "by any means necessary" mentality, too. I looked at my job and said, "What do *I* need to do to accomplish my goal?" Me, me, me. My concerns always revolved around that one word: *me*. My attitude was, "I'll go and get business. You all knock it out and take care of everything else."

I didn't care about the other aspects of the business. Dustin hired me to do a job, and I was going to do it. I did it so well that the company could barely keep up. Multiple times, we had to turn away multimillion-dollar deals because we didn't have the capacity or the people to keep up with the pace of my sales.

I did such a great job that Dustin promoted me to executive vice president of sales and marketing and gave me a team to run. Now I had to look at my department holistically. The "me" mentality shifted to "my team." My team, my team, my team. I remember sitting in a meeting with the other executives and saying to them, "*My* team did what we were supposed to do. *My* team brought in the business. You all need to find a way to get your job done."

I thought to myself, *Man, our sales and marketing team could jam business into this place, but if we don't have the right people on the right teams to fulfill the sales we make, then our sales don't matter.* It wasn't my problem then, but it was about to become my problem.

* * *

After serving as the executive vice president of sales and marketing for a year, Dustin asked me to become president. Suddenly, everything was my responsibility. From overseeing the balance sheet to the income statements, to managing benefits, to planning and executing the company's growth—everything fell on my plate.

I remember looking at the financials for the whole company, and it hit me like a ton of bricks. *I was responsible for everything.* And I realized for the first time, I couldn't do everything by myself. I needed help.

And even more, I couldn't get great people to work with me if everything was about me doing it all by myself. I had to not only get great people around me, but I also had to make them great. I had to teach them. I had to help them excel at their jobs just as well as I excelled in mine.

For most of my career, my success hinged on my discipline, my work ethic, my hustle, and my grind. I rose through the ranks and made money because of how hard I worked at developing my talents and abilities. I looked out for me and only me. In the hardscrabble world I grew up in and the professional ones I ventured into, that's how I survived—how *everyone* survived. It was the only way.

Except at Headspring, it wasn't just about me, and it wasn't just about my sales and marketing team; it was about our whole company. Everyone on the team needed to work together if we wanted to really succeed.

My perspective shifted from, "How can *I* succeed?" to "How can I help *everyone* to succeed?"

I give Dustin a lot of credit for teaching me about the concept of culture and how to foster it in the organization. Many leaders mistakenly think culture is about offering free gym memberships or, "We've got beer in the cooler for you." Or, they believe it's about having foosball tables or cool, relaxing chairs to hang out in.

That is some bullshit. Culture is not the outside appearance of cool and fun. Culture is about the relationships people have with one another and with the organization as a whole. It's how you treat individuals and how you value their contributions to the organization. It's about honest communication from the top down and acting with integrity.

Until Headspring, I worked in industries that lacked integrity. When people walked into the consumer finance office, we knew their financial position in life, yet we still refinanced their loans, we still put them back in a hole—because it made us money. When we sold and packaged mortgages, we sold to people we knew would struggle to make payments. We didn't even care if they had jobs, as long as we could get them approved for the loan. We did this because we wanted to make money. Yes, the work was legal, but it didn't make what we were doing right. And it wasn't about a team mentality or working together to succeed. Everyone in those industries looked out for themselves.

I saw a new world at Headspring—a world where people did work together, where team work was fostered and success shared. Dustin introduced me to the world of a positive team culture.

Then, like everything else in my life, I learned it inside and out and tweaked it to make it stronger. To do this, I started with something I knew well: greeting people and building relationships with them. I made it a point to know every employee's first and last name and three pieces of information about them, even when we employed well over a hundred people. I'd stop and ask how their vacations were and then listen when they responded. Or I'd ask them how they were doing after their grandmother's funeral. I'd ask about their children and then fire off their names to show that I listened, that I'm present with them.

People love to feel that they're a part of something, but even more importantly, they want to feel respected and cared for by leadership. When you can do these things, that's when you start to build a team. Once you have a team in place, you can start to build an environment where people realize the guy at the top isn't in it just to boost the bottom line. What I learned was yes, we were a for-profit company, and I would never stray from that. But I could increase the bottom line by increasing people's happiness, their engagement, and their interactions with one another by showing them that I truly cared about each of them *and* the company. I did all of this by building relationships.

It wasn't about faking the emotions or bullshitting people to manipulate them into thinking that I cared. It was about genuinely caring and seeing everyone as a person, not just as a tool designed to advance a career. This wasn't that hard for me. I do care about people. I had just never combined caring about people with business and teamwork.

I watched how people performed at extraordinary levels when they were valued as human beings, when their passion for learning and their drive for excellence was encouraged and supported.

And this isn't just about the "important" and "talented" people in the company. It goes all the way up and down. I remember one woman who was part of the building's cleaning crew. Like clockwork, she showed up between three and three-twenty in the afternoon, every day. And she always arrived smiling, even though she had to clean the restrooms. I never saw her in a bad mood. For Christmas, I bought her a gift to show her that I valued her. She wasn't the chief architect or one of those highly valued software engineers, but we still needed her, and she deserved my respect.

Part of that was personal for me, too. I had real love for this woman because of how much she reminded me of my mom and myself. Here I was, the president of this company, and I remembered—I started my journey doing what she did: cleaning toilets.

No one ever gave me anything when I was cleaning toilets, but you know what? I can be better than that. I can look at her as what she is—a person, struggling to make it—and I can give her some help. I can show her that she matters and her work matters.

I have to be honest: it felt great, too. To be able to help someone, especially in a place where no one helped me, made me feel good.

No, my act didn't change my past, but it helped me feel better about it. Maybe I healed a little, too.

* * *

Not only did I learn to build a team at Headspring, but I also learned to be part of a team. At least three times a week, I would walk around the office floor observing the Headspring team. On their desks, I saw pictures of their families, vacations, and gifts they likely bought for birthdays and holidays. I smiled as I observed them stooped over their computers, typing emails or talking into their headsets. I may have been responsible for the entire company, but every person was responsible for their job and their own success. And these people owned it. They earned the paychecks they received every two weeks for the work they put in.

Without fail, seeing the impact on their professional and

personal lives made me proud. It was the same emotion I felt when one night, Dustin's wife raised her glass to me and my wife over dinner and said, "Thank you for helping us to pay off our home."

Before Headspring, my actions impacted only me. But now, my decisions, my work ethic, my hustle, and my deep passion to be the best leader I could be weren't just about me anymore. My skills helped to contribute to vacations, new homes, Christmas gifts, and bicycles for a child's birthday. My work was having a real impact on the quality of people's lives, not just my own. I was helping people to accomplish their goals, and that meant something to me.

Knowing this, knowing the impact I could have on the company and people's lives, only drove me to work harder. My philosophy of "by any means necessary" stopped. I stopped the dogged pursuit of making money for only myself, and replaced it with, "How can we grow?"; "How can we grow the company, grow the bottom line, grow each team member?"; and, "How can I help people to grow their lives, too, in a positive way?"

* * *

My time at Headspring taught me more than the importance of culture. It taught me about giving back. It was during my tenure with the company that I began to mentor the youth I mentioned earlier in the book who were caught in the juvenile detention system and trying to transition back into society.

It all started with backpacks. I saw someone walk into the office with a backpack full of school supplies for their kid. It was painful for me to see that. I almost wanted to cry. Here I was, the president of a big software company, getting upset over school supplies. I thought I was going crazy.

But then, I thought about it, and it made sense.

Do you remember in school, the poor kid, the one who never had any school supplies? That was me. And it sucked. It sucked to sit in class and see another kid with a full bag of school supplies while you have nothing. It sucked to see kids with different clothes on every day. The jeans I was going to wear the next day were the same jeans I was going to wear every day.

When I went to school, I had nothing except my clothes. NOTHING. I remembered sitting next to classmates who had all the markers, the pencils, and the cool backpacks. I'd have to raise my hand and ask the teacher for the supplies. It was a horrible feeling being that kid. I remember them giving us our locker assignments, and thinking to myself, *Why am I getting a locker? I ain't got nothing to put in it.* I remember in sixth grade, when I was with my dad, I showed up to school with nothing.

Well, I thought to myself, *I can solve that now*. I couldn't solve it for myself back in the sixth grade, but I had the power to solve it for kids who were going through the same pain now.

I got the idea to start a backpack drive for kids in the worst schools in Austin. I went online and found a list of the poorest schools in the city, the schools that had the highest percentage of kids on free lunch. One school had 99.9 percent of its students receiving free lunch.

I announced to the Headspring team that I was holding a backpack drive, and for every backpack that they brought in filled with school supplies and clothes, I would personally match it. The team brought in thirty backpacks, and true to my word, I matched it. So we collected sixty fully stocked bags and donated them to the school.

The next year, I talked to Dustin. I wanted to go bigger, and he agreed. We found the five schools with the highest percentage of free lunches, and then we went to our clients and the public. We told everyone that we, as a company, would match one-for-one every backpack donated with school supplies.

The final tally: a whopping 2,700 bags chock full of supplies for the year. In some instances, we were able to donate bags to an entire school. We had so many bags that we had to use Lone Star, the regional version of FedEx and UPS, to deliver them.

When I was the kid who didn't have supplies, I felt the shame and embarrassment. It burned in me. I couldn't do anything about my situation then, but by the time I reached Headspring, I could do something about it. So I did, and just like with the cleaning lady, it felt great. To see those kids happy meant the world to me.

I can't change my past, and I wouldn't want to, but damn, it feels great to change the present for someone suffering or in need.

* * *

I spent five years at Headspring, two and a half as its president. During that period, I helped the company grow from thirteen people sitting on metal folding chairs, and me making calls from a storage closet in a tiny office in Austin, to well over a hundred team members spread between four offices (one in Austin, one in Houston, one in Dallas, and one in Monterrey, Mexico).

I credit my rise through the ranks and the growth of the

company to my humility, my willingness to learn new things, and my hustle. No one outworked me.

From day one, when I was making sales calls from a storage closest, I put in the effort. I was driven. I refused to settle. When I was the business development guy, in my mind, every call I made and email I sent out was worth a million dollars. When most people left the office at five in the evening, I'd stay an extra hour to email and call more prospective clients. With every call and every email, I believed that I was one step closer to finding the next business to sell our services to.

Sales is a numbers game, and you have to go through a ton of no's to get to a yes. Most salespeople give up quickly. Those salespeople considered OK will reach out three to five times to the same person. If they reach out five to seven times, they're considered good. If they reach out nine to eleven times, they're ranked as great. If they want to be phenomenal, they have to reach out thirteen to fifteen times.

I have no problem reaching out thirteen to fifteen times or more to a person. But reaching out that number of times to someone bothers a lot of people; that's why they ask me how I do it. My answer is easy. I live by one premise. When I was a kid and came home from school, I'd ask my mom what we were going to eat for dinner. When she told me we weren't eating because we couldn't afford food, well, that hurt. There is nothing like waking up with an empty belly gnawing at you the next morning. It is the worst feeling in the world to be hungry.

But when I place a sales call and someone says they don't want to do business with me, that doesn't hurt. I'm like, *Fine, I'll find someone else to work with because I can continue to go through as many people as I have to until I find a yes.* There are always alternatives in the sales game.

But when I was at home and Mom told me, "No, you're not going to eat," there were no alternatives. I didn't have another option or another phone call I could place to magically put food on the table.

All it took for me to succeed as a top salesperson was my belief that things could always get better for me and my determination to think bigger. This perspective led me to never quit, to work harder and smarter, to be nice to everyone, to hustle, and to keep learning and growing. That's street hustle turned legal.

In many ways, Headspring was the perfect place for me to bring all the lessons and skills I'd developed throughout my life.

But the successes we experienced at Headspring came

with tremendous sacrifices, too. Shortly before I started at Headspring, I met my wife, Megan. She was with me from when I entered the company through my rise. And during my five years with the company, I took a total of only eleven vacation days—three days for my marriage, two for the birth of my daughter, one for the birth of my son, and the rest were sporadic days here and there. Fortunately, I don't get sick, so zero sick days.

I worked long hours and obsessively read and studied business books and leaders. It goes back to watching my mom raise me as a single mother. She couldn't afford to take vacations; she had to keep going. She never stopped working hard, so I kept going and made sacrifices, too. I've had no regrets. All those long days, weekends, and late nights have been worth it to me.

It was especially worthwhile for me when Headspring began appearing on lists for Best Places to Work in Austin and Texas.

* * *

Fifteen hundred people crowded the hotel ballroom waiting to celebrate the annual Best Places to Work in Texas awards. Each year, companies in Texas are ranked based on employee happiness and engagement. Employees have to take a survey that includes a series of questions, such as,

"How likely are you to work in the company in two years?";
"How likely are you to refer a friend to the company?"; "How
happy are you with the management?"; and, "How happy
are you with the decisions that are made?"

Headspring was one of the top companies selected for the
third year in a row. The previous year, we took home number
six, and the year before that, number eight. This is out of all
Texas-based companies. The two years prior to those wins,
Headspring had appeared on the Best Places to Work in Austin
list, but this was for all of Texas, and well, it's a damn big state.

Dustin and I sat listening, as patiently as possible, as the
numbers ticked down. Twenty-five, twenty-four...fifteen,
fourteen...nine, eight. When I heard another company
called for number eight, I remember thinking, *OK, great.*
Beautiful. We passed a previous marker. Then they get to
number six, which we won the previous year, and they
announced another company. *Great!* I thought. *We were*
headed to our personal best. Number five. It wasn't Headspring. *Please, let us make the top three, please,* I prayed.
I really wanted number one, but cracking the top three
would be OK, too.

Number four...Headspring.

It wasn't the placement I had wanted—I always want number

one—but it was better than our ranking the previous year. I was happy when Dustin leaned over and reminded me that this recognition happened under my watch.

Who would have thought that with my background—the abuse, the poverty, the lack of education, the stints in juvenile detention, and the racism I experienced—I would be leading a company voted one of the best places to work in all of Texas three years in a row?

I sat there smiling. I smiled for the hard work, dedication, and commitment that the Headspring team put in every day. I smiled for my own rise at Headspring, from selling our services while sitting in a storage closet to growing a company with over a hundred employees in four offices.

I smiled for the boy I once was—the boy who sat next to his mother on the bus, the boy who plucked half-eaten sandwiches from the school trash cans, the boy who learned about pizza delivery only when he was fifteen years old, the boy who had his high school diploma presented to him by the school janitor.

I smiled for my mom—my hardworking, devoted, loving mother. The woman who was my protector, who loved me, who never gave up on me, who found a way to rescue me from the hell that was my life in Dayton.

And I smiled for my journey, all of it, and for what would come next.

ELEVEN

There and Back Again

I GOT THE CALL A FEW MONTHS BEFORE I STARTED THIS BOOK: my father had passed away.

My first reaction was not to go back to Dayton for my father's funeral. But at the urging of my wife, my mother, and my friend, Tucker, I decided to make the trip.

I went because I realized attending the funeral wasn't just about burying my dad or about paying respects to him. It was about burying thirty years of anger, rage, and shame.

It was time to face my past so I could let it go.

Coincidentally, my mother was visiting me when I heard the news. I broke his death to her. She took it harder than I did, but then, she had fonder memories of him than I did.

My mom asked if I wanted her to go with me. I said no. It was a trip I wanted and needed to take alone.

DAYTON

My father's service was standing room only. So many people showed up for him. Hundreds.

I listened as pimps, drug dealers, and others shared stories and memories about my father. I heard all these pimps talk about him in such glowing ways.

My dad's nickname was Boobie. They said things like, "Boobie taught me the game. Boobie taught me how to hustle. Boobie taught me how to dress."

Just over and over, all this praise for him. People had these great things to say about when he opened a nightclub back in the day. They laughed, shed a few tears, and celebrated his life.

I had a hard time believing what I was hearing. I thought to myself, *Ain't this some shit? He didn't do anything for me or* any *of his twenty-three kids, and you guys are here celebrating him? I got none of what you all are talking about.*

I didn't share their memories. I didn't have their stories. What I remembered was being a young boy, falling asleep standing at the window, waiting for the man who never came to pick me up.

What I remembered was the man who took a two-week trip to England that turned into eleven months.

What I remembered was bouncing from abusive home to abusive home, caring for my brother and sisters alone, and going in and out of juvenile detention.

As a father now, I just can't understand what my dad was thinking. Why did he do this? Why did he choose that life?

He had twenty-three kids, so obviously, his actions weren't directed just at me. It wasn't personal. I didn't do anything to cause him to treat me the way he did. But damn, I still shake my head wondering how any man could do what my father did to me and his other children.

I waited for a family member to go up and speak about him. No one went up. Not one family member, not any of his sisters, not his brother, none of the other kids said one word.

I finally thought, *To hell with this. I'm going to go say something.* So I walked up there and I said, "I'm one of his twenty-three."

Everybody started laughing because everyone knew he had twenty-three kids—confirmed.

> *"I had no clue my father had this impact on this many people. I've heard all these great memories you all have with my father. I'm glad for you.*
>
> *I don't share those same great memories. The memory I have of my father is being a little kid, no more than five or six, and him saying he's coming to pick me up, and he would never show up. I'd stand in that window for hours waiting for him to show up. He never came.*
>
> *He abandoned me more times than I can count—one time for eleven months. Yeah, you heard that right.*
>
> *So I'm here today because, be it heaven or hell or wherever he's watching us from right now, I didn't want him waiting for me to show up. I didn't want him wondering if I was going to show up. I didn't want him to have to wait for me, like I waited for him all those years before. I'm not him. I didn't leave him hanging. I showed up.*

Dad, this is what it looks like when you take care of your responsibilities."

I walked off...and the room erupted in applause.

I have to admit, that reaction shocked me. I wasn't expecting that kind of response.

* * *

Dad died penniless. All that hustling, all that money he made, and yet he died flat broke. In fact, he owed people money.

Like I've said, there are no retired pimps. He couldn't even afford to pay for his own funeral, and no one, other than my little half brother Mario, the one I potty trained, offered to pay.

Although I hadn't spoken to my father or been back to Dayton in thirty years, I decided to pay the $3,800 funeral tab.

I gave, once again, where I never got. But this time, it was OK. Paying for his funeral helped me in a way that I never imagined it could.

When I handed my Black Card to the funeral home, I felt proud. I was proud of the man I had become, of the life I had built for myself, and the family that was waiting for me in Austin.

There I was, back in Dayton, Ohio—a dead city, rust belt, broken, poor, dirty, run-down, just awful. I was a discarded kid from that failed city. When Uncle Bobby put me on that plane, I left Dayton with a few shirts and pants stuffed into my mom's old raggedy suitcase.

Yet, thirty years later, I returned being chauffeured in a town car, dressed in my custom clothes, and wearing a watch that cost more than most homes. I paid the $3,800 for my dad's funeral as if it were nothing.

Who would have thought my life would look like this? I kept thinking to myself in Dayton.

When I paid my father's funeral bill, it was as though I was in a conversation with him. *"Dad, look at what I just did. You didn't pick me up, yet I'm the one who came through in the end to pick you up. I'm here, I won, I've become the better man, and now I'm going home."*

Yes, I was proud of how far I'd come since I had left Dayton all those years ago, but I was also a little bitter.

No, it wasn't mature.

But it was how I felt.

It was my way of proving, to myself at least, that my dad and I were not alike.

* * *

After the funeral, I reconnected with my half brother and two half sisters—Amber's kids, the ones whom I'd cared for when she was out prostituting and doing heroin for days on end. I sat and talked to them on the stoop of a rental home owned by one of my cousins. I watched as cars with rims worth more than the vehicles drove by with their stereos booming. It was like we were in a scene straight from the movie *Boyz in the Hood*.

We talked for a long time. It was hard. I shared a lot of stories about their mother with them, and they shared stories of the horrific experiences they went through with their mother after I left. It was bad shit. Really bad. Worse than most of what I went through.

What blew me away was that they still had pictures of me, and their childhood memories of me were so positive. They told me that some of their best memories from childhood were of the times they had spent with me.

Hearing them say that I was at the center of some of their

best memories shook me to the core. They were so young when we were all together, and for them to remember those times clawed at a space deep inside of me.

My childhood was rough, it was tough, but at least I had my mom for a good part of it. They didn't have anyone. They lived through hell, and hearing that I was someone to them, someone they cherished, loved, and remembered fondly, broke me open.

I felt such aching guilt that I wasn't there to protect them like my mom protected me, that I wasn't there to care for them like my mom cared for me. Hearing them talk about me as a positive, loving memory brought back those years I lived off and on with my father. During those moments of emptiness, I would remember my mom, her love, and her warmth.

How could my sisters and brother remember me the way I had remembered my mom? I wondered.

I know that it was never my responsibility to take care of them, but a part of me still feels like it was. I can't help but wonder what pain or anguish I could have helped to prevent or at least lessen if I had been with them.

We shared many stories together that day. I even opened

up to my sister about the one story I thought I would never share with anyone.

"Hey, there's something that I'm going to share with you that I've not shared with anyone," I told her. "No one knows what I'm about to tell you. I've carried this with me since I was nine years old." I gave her the whole story. The story I told earlier in the book, about how when she wouldn't stop crying and I threw her on the sofa. And I said to her, as sincerely as I've ever said it in my life, "I am *so* sorry."

She gave me a hug and she told me that it's not my fault. She said, "Our mom was fucked up. That's not even close to as bad as some of the stuff we went through. There's nothing to apologize for. I have nothing but great memories of the things that you did for us. I can only imagine the things that you did shelter us from."

She gave me a hug, and we cried together.

I cried a lot that day, with them.

I don't know why I can't shake that story. Every time I think about it, I get upset. I can tell every one of the stories in this book and be OK, and I have found a lot of peace in doing this book. But that story, I can't shake.

It lingers with me, haunting me. I was just a scrawny nine-year-old who was away from his mom for the first time ever. I was confused, scared, afraid, and forced to care for a child whom I had no business caring for. I had no clue what to do, and no one was there to show or tell me what I was supposed to do. I felt powerless in that moment, a moment where the stakes were really high. I was forced to care for a helpless child, to protect her, to comfort her, and to give her what she needed.

It's a feeling that I still carry with me to this day. That's why I'm passionate about studying everything and anything I can. I always want to make sure that I know what I'm doing so I never feel lost, confused, scared, and powerless again.

I've run from that particular story for thirty-five years. That story itself is part of the reason why I'm still running when I'm so far past the goal line, so far from my life in Dayton.

At least twice a month, I drive past Seventh Street in Austin, where the homeless linger and where the Salvation Army is, and I look at the people. I see them and I think to myself, *Man, you were about half a step away from being one of those people.*

Maybe that's part of it. Maybe it's that I realize I could have ended up like my dad or like Amber and had that horrific way of life, of not caring. Maybe that scares me. Maybe I study so hard and work so hard to make sure I will never be like them.

I struggle with the success I have. I feel guilty that I left my three half siblings behind. I feel ashamed that I made it out and they didn't. I got out, and I left them behind with Amber. And lots of bad stuff happened to them—sexual abuse, rape, violence, drug addiction, all of that. I know I went through a lot of that, too, but they had it worse.

And it's not just them. I know so many people from Dayton who had it as messed up or worse than me. Sometimes it's hard for me to accept that I've achieved success and climbed out of that hole when I know there are a lot of people who are still trapped in the hood.

Every day, I ask myself, *Do I deserve all this success? Do I deserve for my life to be nice? Do I deserve to be able to tell my story in a book? Do I deserve to have earned millions of dollars and to pay $3,800 for a funeral without blinking an eye? Do I really deserve the family, the career, and the life that I'm living?*

I walked the same streets in Dayton as my brother and sisters, and all my other siblings and cousins. I experienced the same horrors, but why did I get out? Why me and not any of them? Why do I have this success?

I struggle with these questions every day.

On the day of my father's funeral, sitting on the porch stoop next to my sisters and brother, I looked around, I remembered where I came from, and I cried. I cried for my life, for their lives, and for the childhoods we endured. I cried for our struggles and traumas and the ones those in the hood still endure.

SELF-MADE

Looking back on my life, I can't remember how many times people mistook my race and I never corrected them. Sometimes people assumed I was Hispanic. The way I saw it, if I needed to be Hispanic, then I was Hispanic. Or if somebody cracked a black joke, and I was in an audience where it was going to advance me in some way, I didn't admit that I was half black. I just said nothing.

There were even times when I didn't want to be white. If I was with a group of black kids, I didn't want to admit that my mother was white. I was embarrassed because I knew they'd make fun of me. If I was with black people, I considered myself black. If I was with white people, I considered myself white.

When I met people in a business context, many of them

assumed I had an MBA because of how successful and knowledgeable I was. They'd ask me where I went to school, but instead of correcting them, I sidestepped the question and continued to talk business. Most people never pressed the issue and assumed I must have gone to a good school if I was this humble about it. If people wanted to assume I had an MBA and that helped me advance professionally, then I'd let them. I never wanted to tell anyone that I lacked an MBA, let alone a four-year degree, and that I barely passed high school.

I never tried to actively deceive people. I never lied. If I was directly asked, I would tell the truth. I just wanted to fit in. I needed to blend in. I needed to manipulate my situation because life taught me that my race did matter. I thought that my lack of formal education credentials would hold me back. I thought that people would judge me based on my past and how I grew up as a poor, mixed-race kid from the dirty streets of Dayton.

I never told people about my horrible childhood. I never admitted that I grew up in Dayton. I dressed immaculately, and I changed my name from JeVon to JT. I did this because I knew how the game worked. I knew that people were quick to judge, and if they knew certain things about my past, their impression of me would change. And that change, even if they weren't aware of it, would hurt me in my career.

And that was something I couldn't risk because my career and my success is what kept me away from the streets of Dayton, away from that lifestyle, away from my past.

One time, after telling my wife, Megan, a story about this, she looked at me and said, "You've had to be a chameleon your whole life. You read the situation around you and change your color and shape to match it, to fit in, to be protected from predators. But you don't have to do that anymore. You're safe now."

That really hit me hard. I had never thought about it like that—that my perceptive abilities were a way to survive and that my adaptability helped me change who I was to fit any situation.

* * *

Another time, I was telling a story to my friend about a business meeting I had. I was presenting a proposal to a major New York investment bank, and the boardroom was full of senior directors of the firm. I got the meeting because my mentor was a former C-level executive there, and he'd connected me to them.

After I was done with the presentation, we were all talking business, everything from Amazon's strategy to bond investments. One of the guys looked at me and said, "Ivy League MBA?"

As he said that, one of the other guys kept talking, so I pretended I didn't hear his comment. I focused on the other guy and kept answering his question.

A few minutes later, there was another lull in the conversation, and a different guy asked me the same question: "Which Ivy did you get your MBA from?"

I guess asking this question is a clique thing at this bank, because this was the second time they asked me in a matter of minutes. Again, instead of answering them, I redirected the conversation.

We kept talking, and then I got asked a third time, point blank, where I went to school. I froze, panicked that I was going to have to address my education, to admit that I had no education at all.

Then the main guy in the room said, "You're a friend of our former VP, right?" That saved me. Once it was established how I got the meeting (through my mentor, who is one of the most respected men on Wall Street), no one gave a damn about any Ivy League MBA, and no one brought it up again.

As I finished this story, my friend asked, "Dude, what are you afraid of? Why were you panicked?"

I admitted I was afraid that I'd be exposed, that they would know my knowledge is not from an Ivy League school. My knowledge isn't even from a junior college. My knowledge is because I wake up every day at 4:00 a.m. and I teach myself what's going on in the world. I taught myself how to look at balance sheets and quarterly earnings of publicly traded companies, and that's where my education came from.

My friend flipped it on me. "No, man, you handled this all wrong. Next time, do the opposite. When you get that question, go directly into it. Tell them straight up, not only did you not get an MBA, you don't have a college degree. Hell, tell them you had to go to summer school to graduate high school, and you were so bad at school, you got your diploma from the janitor."

The look on my face must have shown him how confused I was at this.

"JT, don't you understand? All the arrogance and bluster and bragging from those bankers is to mask their deep insecurity. Every single Ivy League MBA wonders, deep down, whether they deserve it. They wonder if they're nothing without their fancy degree. They just go from fancy schools to fancy banks to fancy corporations, and they never once take real risks in their lives. They don't test themselves, so they don't know who they are. You never had that luxury.

Your whole life is nothing but tests and risks and beating them to succeed."

I nodded, following along.

"That's why they cared about your degree—they wanted to know where you fit in their hierarchy. But you aren't from their hierarchy. You have the ultimate business trump card. *You're truly self-made.*"

This was a pivotal moment in my life. It was like the skies opened and a totally different light came down on me, and I saw myself differently.

I realized, maybe for the first time, I did this; I created this life myself. I didn't have to be ashamed of not having the right degrees. I'd done something far more impressive than being good at school—I learned how to be good at life.

Hell, yeah! I *am* self-made!

This realization freed me. I no longer have to pretend to be something I'm not or let people have assumptions of me that aren't true. I can own everything about myself and be who I am because I made it on my terms.

Those two conversations—with my wife and with my

friend—combined with my trip back to Dayton, helped me to accept who I am.

They helped me accept that I am JeVon Thomas McCormick.

That I grew up on the streets of Dayton, Ohio.

That I'm half white *and* I'm half black.

That I grew up so poor we couldn't afford the *o* and the *r*. We were just *po*.

That my mother was an orphan.

That my father was a drug dealer and a pimp.

That I was abused and neglected as a child.

That I spent time in juvie.

That I don't have an MBA.

That I don't even have a college degree.

And I'm OK with all of this. I'm OK with myself and my life.

I'm not ashamed of my past, where I came from, or what

I've gone through to get where I am any longer. My past and all my experiences are where I came from and will always be a part of who I am.

But it's not all that I am. I decided to be more. I decided to believe in myself, to believe that I could have a better I life, and to do the work necessary to get it.

I am self-made.

(I mean that I'm as self-made as a person can be. I still had help from a lot of people, and I don't discount that at all, of course.)

* * *

When I was in Dayton, I saw bits and pieces of my past and caught glimpses of what my life could have been. I could have been living in the hood or trapped in man prison. I could have been broke or living off the system. I could have been dealing drugs, maybe women as well, or dead.

But that isn't my life. By the grace of God and my own hard work, determination, and hustle, I made it. I climbed from the lowest socioeconomic rung to the highest.

As I flew back home to Austin from my father's funeral, I stared out the window and processed all the complicated emotions I felt on my trip. Since the day I left Dayton as a teen, I tried as hard as I could to never go back. I ran as fast as I could away from Dayton, away from my father, away from the man I could have become, and away from the pain.

My flight connected in Houston. As we descended, I saw the homes laid out beneath us, and I flashed back.

I remembered the rides my dad once took me on when we lived in Houston. I remembered pressing my nose to the window and gazing at the mansions, the luxury cars, and the men who wore those crisp, tailored suits.

Then it hit me: I was one of those men I used to watch in Houston, and I was living in one of those homes that my ten-year-old self longed for.

I've come a long way from those days when my father stopped in the middle of the highway to beat a woman, and the days when Mom and I had only lima beans to eat for dinner. Today, I live in a beautiful home, in a gated community, where my master bathroom is bigger than the apartment I grew up in.

I even have a pond in my backyard where I watch ducks and huge white birds (my mom says the birds are egrets;

10-5-71

Miss Anna-Marie McCormick
945 N. Broadway - Apt. 3
Dayton, Ohio 45407

Welf

Re: Self - patient
9-25-71 to 9-29-71

DETACH AND RETURN THIS STUB WITH YOUR CHECK

DATE	DESCRIPTION	CHARGES	CREDITS	LAST AMOUNT IS BALANCE DUE
	AMOUNT OF PREVIOUS BILL RENDERED			
10-5-71	Balance Due			$422.90

THE MIAMI VALLEY HOSPITAL

This is the receipt the hospital gave my mom for my birth. See the "Welf" tag on the left-hand side? Yeah, that is because she was on welfare. How wrong is it that I was literally tagged from birth as a welfare kid?

That's me and my mom when I was four. This is one of the only photos we have together from my childhood.

I keep this receipt framed at my desk to remind me where I came from. In case you can't read it, it's a receipt for rent. We were so poor, my mom could only afford a ten-dollar payment on the $145 monthly rent.

This is the abandoned house where Amber left me, my half brother, and two half sisters. I visited it when I went back to Dayton for my father's funeral, and I wept in the streets. It was hard.

This is the back of the weekly motel where Amber left me with my crying six-month-old half sister.

This is the suitcase the orphanage gave my mom when she left, and she passed down to me. It's the suitcase I hugged while I was homeless, sleeping in bus stops. It's the suitcase I left Dayton with at fifteen. I still have it.

This is my dad. Could be the very definition of a '70s pimp. Like I said, he dressed well.

This is my dad with a "colleague."

This is me with my dad's best friend, back from his pimp and hustler days.

Like I said, all the old-school pimps and hustlers came out for my dad's funeral. I had to get a picture with some of them together. Otherwise, I'm not sure anyone in my life would believe this.

I call them cranes) swim. Sometimes I spy deer drinking from the water, too.

We've lived in our home for three years, yet I still wake up and look out the bay window in the master bedroom and shake my head, thinking, *Damn, I have a pond with ducks in my backyard.*

Some people may glance at nature, not quite seeing it. I see it because who would have thought someone like me would ever enjoy such a view?

Every morning, I wake up between 4:00 a.m. and 4:30 a.m. I spend the first hour and a half of my day studying my craft. I want to be a great leader, great in business, and great at investing. Monday through Friday, an hour and a half is dedicated to learning how to do these things. Then I spend thirty minutes thinking about how I'm going to apply what I studied that day. After I finish studying, I spend at least an hour going to the gym, then an hour or so with the family for breakfast. Then I go to work, do my thing, come home, and spend another two hours with my family. Before I go to bed, I read even more.

When it's just me wandering around the house early in the morning or late at night, I spy my kids' toys scattered on the floor. Some people may get frustrated; not me. I smile.

They get to have toys and a great life. Those toys remind me that my kids won't ever have to go through what I did.

I watch how men and women run through our gated community, and I think how amazing it is that they're running for health and enjoyment. Back in Dayton, people didn't run for fun; they ran from bullets.

Today, I don't have to worry about copays or affording doctors' visits; I have health insurance. I don't have to stress about catching the bus on time; I have a car. When I want to watch television, I flick on our ninety-inch television hanging on the wall. Do I need such a big screen? No, but I've worked hard to afford one, and it's another reminder of how far I've come. Growing up, my mom had a nineteen-inch, black-and-white television with a broken antenna that barely showed three channels.

I no longer have to worry about affording the basics. Growing up, Mom made us use a bar of soap until it disintegrated. Now, when a bar of soap starts getting down to a small sliver, I toss it out and reach underneath the bathroom sink to grab another one from the stack. When I open the bathroom closet, I see three to five bottles of my favorite lotion and razors stored in mass quantity.

When I was a kid, I never knew if there would be food in

the refrigerator when I opened it. But now, I open the fridge or the pantry and it's always stocked, especially with chocolate milk.

I remember the days of going to school in Dayton. The schools were so bad that I wasn't allowed to take home my books. But today, I'm the president and CEO of a book publishing company. I even have my own book.

When I remember my childhood days, when I think about how I carried my mom's suitcase with me through the school halls, and how I scraped by to get my high school diploma in summer school, all that echoes in my mind is, *Who knew that I would get there? Who knew that I'd live the phenomenal life I'm living today?*

I knew—that's who. I believed I could achieve financial success, that I could create a bigger and better life for myself.

When I smile thinking about my life today, I smile because I've attained it.

I easily navigate the world of business, as comfortable negotiating deals in boardrooms with the upper echelon of business as I am mentoring youth just out of juvenile detention and living in halfway homes. Both environments make up my story and have shaped the man I am today.

I never forget where I came from. My past, all that I've over-come, makes me appreciate the good moments in my life. I don't take those or my successes in life for granted, and I certainly don't feel entitled to my wealth or achievements.

All of us can find something, someone, or society itself to blame for our challenges. But I decided to not let my past or any experience I've endured stop me.

When I'm with the boys from the halfway house, I tell them, "You get to decide who you are going to become. You will move forward in your life; tomorrow will come regardless. The only question is who that person will be, and ultimately, it's up to you to decide that."

I've created the life I once dreamed of—I have a loving wife, amazing children, a beautiful home, a successful career, and financial freedom.

I am one of those men in those homes in Houston whom I used to dream about.

I got there.

TWELVE

Tragic Endings and Hard Truths

———

DECEMBER 2017

This chapter was written a year after the book was published.

But it's not a post script. This is very much a part of my story.

Most of what's in this chapter should have been in the original version of the book, but I wasn't ready to face these truths then.

I am now.

Let me start on the night of the book release party, on January 20, 2016.

This should have been a celebration. The entire Scribe Media (formerly Book In A Box) tribe was there, along with several of our freelancers. My wife and children and many of our friends were all celebrating the book. Everything was set up to be a special night.

Everyone who mattered in my life was there. Except one person:

My mother.

She had turned down my offer to come to the book release party.

I tried and tried to get her to come, but she wouldn't come. She talked about her health—which was not good—and she talked about how she didn't like to fly, and all kinds of excuses. I offered to charter a private jet to get her to come. No dice.

You know how when someone gives you lots of reasons for something, they aren't telling you the real reason.

Now, the day of the release party came, and not only was she not there...but she was missing.

I mean this literally. She fit the legal definition of a missing person.

My stepfather had called me that morning and told me that she'd taken $3,000 in cash, a car, and one of his guns, and disappeared. No note, no call, nothing. Vanished. He called the cops and reported her missing. He was incredibly upset.

I didn't tell anyone, except my wife. On the way to the launch event, we had this conversation:

Megan: "Are you excited about your book launch tonight?"

JT: "I hate to say it, but no. I'm not."

Megan: "Why?"

JT: "It's hard to be excited when you're about to put your whole life out to the public, and you don't even know if the person who supported you the most is even alive."

I went to the book release party, and honestly, I was awful. I just went through the motions. I gave a half-hearted speech, I put on a fake smile during the pictures, and I can hardly even remember anything about that day to write about it.

Don't get me wrong, I held it all in well—because I am good at hiding my emotions—but I was devastated on the inside.

As far as I knew, my mom was dead.

And part of me couldn't help but feel like it was my fault.

*   *   *

After the book came out, I got a lot of positive feedback from readers. But there was one comment that wasn't entirely positive, one that I heard over and over from people:

I wanted more explanation of your relationship with your mom. I felt like you glossed over that and idealized it.

People said that same thing over and over in different ways. They loved how honest I was in talking about my dad, but they felt like I idolized my mom too much. I made her out to be a saint, when she was clearly flawed in some fundamental ways. And they felt like I wasn't willing to explore those areas, whereas I was willing to be so raw and honest in every other area.

This comment shocked and confused me at first. I really thought I was being as open as I could be about my relationship with her.

But as I thought about it, I realized there was a lot of truth to that.

In fact, the more I thought about it, the more I realized it was right.

I hadn't been as open about my emotions surrounding her as I thought.

At this point, you've read the book. You might even feel the same way. And if so, you're right, I was pretty honest about my dad, and did give her a pass. More than a few times where I left unanswered questions about her.

Why did I do that?

It wasn't on purpose. God knows my writing team at Scribe Media (formerly Book In A Box) pushed me to open up on everything I could.

I guess I just wasn't ready.

I was very excited as I wrote my book. It was a really wonderful process for me to finally get all of this out, to tell my story and to finally explore so much of the painful parts of my childhood. Hard, yes, but also very rewarding to know

I was leaving a legacy like this for my children, and maybe helping some other people too.

I wanted to share this experience with my mom. We'd been through this together. I wanted this book to be both of ours. Our celebration.

She did not share my enthusiasm for the book. In fact, she was petrified of the book.

"Am I gonna look bad?" She would break down into tears, "Am I gonna look like I was a bad mother? Am I gonna look like I didn't take care of you? I have not really accomplished much in life. The one piece that I feel I accomplished in life was I raised you. I'm proud of you, what you've become, and I don't wanna look like I failed with that."

"No, Mom, you won't." I would take parts of the book and show her, "Mom, the way the book is written, you look like the greatest mom in the world. Why are you stressing?"

She told me she felt that she failed during the time period where she wasn't there for me. She said she didn't want people to ask the obvious questions, like, "How did this woman not take care of her child? Where was this woman for her son?"

Those are the pieces she wanted to know. She asked me, "Did you put in there that I didn't know you left Houston? That your dad took you without telling me?"

I tried to tell her I did. "Mom, the stories clearly laid out what happened. I know what the fuck happened and how I ended up with dad and you didn't know I left. It is documented in detail."

I also didn't understand who she was worried would read this. My mom has minimal friends and no family. I asked her, "Who are you worried about judging you?"

She didn't have a great answer, she just said, "I'm not really concerned for anyone else, I just don't want to be thought of as a bad parent."

I know after reading this book, you are probably just as confused as me. Why would she feel like she failed me? I'm clearly successful. I adore her. Why would she feel that she failed?

I don't know.

Maybe there are elements about my childhood that she won't tell me. Maybe she did some things that she isn't proud of, things that make her feel guilty and ashamed.

I honestly don't know what they are. She never told me. Everything I know about my past is in this book.

But the book is not everything *she* knows.

It seems pretty obvious to me, especially now, that she harbors a lot of guilt. Even though I've tried to tell her that she doesn't need to, she still does.

So yeah, those conversations I had with her probably did affect the book.

Quite frankly, they did affect it. They probably made it worse.

I think I wouldn't even let myself examine the idea that my mom wasn't a saint. I painted her as perfect, because I wanted her to be perfect, so I made my image of her perfect. And I think she wanted me to see her that way, to hide something she felt guilty about.

Maybe I used my belief in her as a way to hold myself up for years. Maybe I needed to see her as perfect, just as much as she needed to see herself as a good mom.

For most of my life, she was the only person I could know for a fact loved me. Maybe I needed to see her as a saint, as flawless, so I could have something, anything, stable in my life I felt like I could lean on. I idolized her and painted a picture of her in my mind that no one could live up to.

I don't want to make it seem like I have some dirty secrets to let out about my mom. I don't. Like I said, everything that happened that I know of is in the book.

I told you the events that happened. But I think it's pretty clear I wasn't always honest—with myself—about how I felt about them.

* * *

My mom disappeared the day my book came out. From all outward appearances, it looked like she did it intentionally, and did it to take her own life.

In some ways, her wanting to take her own life was not a shock. She'd been sick for a while. I could see the decline and she just wasn't the same person anymore. Her litany of health problems were really starting to take their toll.

She had hepatitis C. Dementia was starting to set in. But the worst was Parkinson's. She shook like crazy, which prevented her from doing all the things that she used to be able to do. She loves to sew and quilt, but she couldn't do it anymore. She was so frustrated that she couldn't make clothes for Ava. I tried to tell her I could buy Ava's clothes, but she didn't care.

On her last visit, only two months before my book came out, she really just didn't feel like my mom. She wasn't the person who got on the bus with me. The woman who played the roles of both mom and dad. The one who showed me both strength and power. Something had fundamentally changed.

On that same visit, she swore to me that she'd never go back to an institution. That she was raised in one, it was hell, and she would die before she went back.

I tried to tell her that I would never let her go back, that I would pay whatever it took to ensure she had top quality in-home care, and between me and her husband, she'd be safe at home. I don't think she believed me.

So even though it was not a complete shock that she wanted to take her own life, I wonder how much of a coincidence it was that all of this happened at the same time as my book release.

I wonder about the symbolism of her abandoning me right before my book launch, when the book would talk about how she abandoned me at another time in my life.

I don't know. It hurts to think about this.

Maybe it wasn't really her. Maybe it was the dementia. Maybe she wanted to go her own way. I can't blame her for that. Even though I would have taken care of her, I don't think she believed me, or would even be able to let me.

Maybe the book was a good thing, and it helped her go.

Given what my mom did read about the book, given what she knew about what I feel and how in depth we went into conversations with me telling her she was a great mom, maybe the book helped her find peace in knowing she was a good mom.

Or maybe there was something else going on.

Maybe she did feel like she failed me as a mother.

In fact, maybe she did. I don't think she did, but it's possible, I guess.

I still think there are things she hasn't told me. They may not even be that bad, but I think they are things she didn't want to face or admit, even to herself.

Maybe the book was too much for her. Maybe the fact that

I idolized her and revered her was too painful, because it made her think about some unrevealed truth that she was too ashamed of.

I don't know what she was thinking. She never told me, and then she disappeared.

But I will say I was very hurt, and very disappointed by how she handled the release of my book. All I wanted was to share this triumph and this joy with her.

But she decided to go her own way.

* * *

As the months passed, with no word from my mother, things got back to normal and settled into a routine. The company kept growing and improving. Megan and I had our third child, Elle.

But I never stopped thinking about my mom. Where was she? What was she doing? Was she even alive or dead?

I talked about this with my wife a lot. I was torn because on one hand, if my mom just showed up one day safe and sound, I would be so fucking pissed.

But then, I would also be so relieved to see her, to know she's alive.

It was such a mind fuck. Which would be worse, to find out she's dead, or to find out she just decided to take herself off the grid for a while?

It's a shitty thing to say about your mom, but I'd actually rather she decided to just take her life.

I mean, I want her alive, but if she decided to end her own life in her own way, I could understand that. There's a logic to that decision. I mean, the timing was fucked, and the way she did it was fucked, but still, it's her life. If she's out, OK, I can understand that.

But what if, instead of that, she's just chilling somewhere? Man, I don't know how I would handle that.

WHAT MAKES ME DIFFERENT?

My mom never really changed much over her life.

My dad tried to go straight. He couldn't handle it. My dad made a lot of money in his life, but still died broke. I am one of twenty-three confirmed kids from my father.

I've often thought about this.

Why me? Why did I succeed, whereas my parents did not? What is different about me?

Was it just luck? Or is there something fundamentally different about me?

I thought about that for a long time.

I think a lot of it comes down to mindset.

My mom has a deep scarcity mindset. Everything with her is about what can go wrong. I'll give you an extreme, but telling, example.

When Megan and I got pregnant, Mom's response was, "Why would you bring a child into this world?"

Megan was disturbed by that comment. I didn't get upset, because I understood her. She still viewed life from what she went through in raising me. I've struggled to accept that I'm successful and that I actually got there in life. My mom never let that go. She still sees herself as a broken orphan from a children's home, and it still fucks her up emotionally. She breaks up every time we talk about it.

Remember, she grew up in an orphanage in the '50s. Those were brutal, awful places. She was molested, she was beat, she was put in solitary confinement for weeks on end. All of that shit affected her throughout her whole life, and she was never able to address it or get past it.

I tried to talk to her about it, and we had some conversations about it. But she never really told me much. Talking about it with her was weird. The best way I can explain it, it's like someone who went to war. They'll give you stories when they want to, but they're not going to go into detail. That's really how it has been with my mom and the children's home. When she was ready to talk about it, she would give you some, but very little, and that's it. She's from that generation that did not talk about their feelings and their pain.

I've thought about the mindset my mom had. How scared she was of everything. How she always thought about the problems. She never strived to do more, because she always had the mindset that "there are people worse off than us."

I gotta be honest, it disgusts me to think in that mindset.

I know it's factually true, but I'm not going to be happy just because other people are worse. I deserve more, I want more, I want to achieve more, and I am willing to work for it. I'm not going to focus on what anyone else is doing, whether they are worse off or better off. No one else's life impacts what mine becomes. I get to make my life.

Maybe I got my mindset from seeing my mom suffer and hold herself back. I ask why for everything. She asked why too, but hers was different. Her why was, "Why did this happen to me? Why did I come from the children's home?" That was her why.

Whereas my why is, "Why can't I have these things? Why can't I live in a $25 million home? Why can't I be in the *Forbes* 400?"

Those are the whys that I choose to focus on.

My mom didn't have anyone to show her anything but that limited mindset. It's all she knew.

But then again, neither did I.

As horrible as my upbringing was, I saw the pockets of life that offered more, and I decided to try for them. The greatest piece ever was when my dad did try to get out of the hustle pimp game and move to Houston. He tried to live a normal life for all of nine months. When I got to drive through River Oaks and see that people lived in homes bigger than the apartment complexes that I lived in, it was very inspiring to me. I'd think, *Okay, they have that, why can't I have it?*

There's nothing that says that I can't have it, at least in my mind. That's the way I looked at it. Those people put their pants on just like I do. They go to sleep just like I do. Yeah, they sleep in a hell of a lot better bed, but they still go to sleep like I do.

If they can do it, it means it can be done.

And if it can be done, I can find a way to do it.

My dad wouldn't put in the work to get there.

And my mom was afraid to reach for it.

But I wasn't afraid. Not of the risk, or the work.

I believe anybody can do what I did. It's all about what you choose to focus on.

*   *   *

They found my mom about a year after my book came out.

She had rented a remote cabin. She stayed there until the

payment ran out. The landlords called the cops, and by the time the cops found her, she was completely disoriented. She had no idea who she even was.

As I write this, she is still alive, but the dementia has taken hold. She doesn't recognize her grandchildren, and she barely even knows who I am.

I wish I could get some more answers from her. Why she acted the way she did when my book came out. What was she afraid of?

I'll never know.

I love my mom. I will always love her.

But she made her choices. She decided to look at life a different way than I do. I can't do anything about that.

I can only let her know I love her, and that I am grateful for everything she did for me.

But I will make sure I don't pass her mindset on to my children.

They will know they can do anything, and be anything, and have anything, as long as they are willing to put in the work necessary. It's not easy to reach high goals, but it's doable.

And now, that is the mindset of my family.

It's Not about Me Anymore

———

*"Touch the hole in your life, and
there flowers will bloom."*

ZEN PROVERB

I'VE STOPPED RUNNING FROM MY PAST, BUT I DON'T
think this means I'm staying still. Not a chance.

I'm proud of the life I lead today. My top priorities are to
be a great follower of God, a great husband, a great father,
and a great leader. Even though I've accomplished a lot
in life and I've traveled so far from where I began, I don't
sit back and rest. I've never said, "OK, that's enough. I've

arrived." No, I haven't arrived; I'm still on my way. My journey continues. Everyone's does.

But now, instead of running away from my pain and my past, I'm running toward something good. My struggle used to be about me only. Me, me, me. I competed with coworkers. I fought to break records. I strove to make millions of dollars. I didn't think about anyone else. I fought for my survival and mine alone.

I don't want that anymore. My dream is no longer that I be one of those people living in the big homes. I have a new dream.

My new dream is that everyone who came from where I came from can live here, too.

I got there...but now I want to go back and bring as many people with me as I can.

TEACHING THE GAME: WE DON'T KNOW WHAT WE DON'T KNOW

I currently mentor youth in the juvenile detention system. I see a lot of problems in that system, but there is one that stands out far above the rest: we don't teach these kids how the game of life works.

When I think about how I got to where I am today, the lesson that sticks out the most is that I learned how to play society's game. However, we don't even tell these kids the game exists, much less what the rules are.

Let me give you an example. When I started mentoring the boys in the halfway house, one of the first things I did was ask the superintendent what the boys needed most.

"They need jobs," he said.

"OK, well, why don't they have them?" I wondered.

"They just haven't been able to get them," he replied, shaking his head.

"Well, why not?" I asked. He had no answer.

I went in to talk with the boys, and the first thing I did was ask them to shake my hand. Their handshakes were weak, and no one made eye contact. Then I asked them to pretend like they were walking into a Burger King to ask for a job application. One of the kids humored me.

"Y'all hirin'?" he said in a bored tone.

Of course these boys haven't been able to get jobs; it's obvious why. No one's going to give them a job when they act like that. They don't know the unspoken rules of how society works. As I like to say, they don't know what they don't know.

If these kids walked in, shook the manager's hand with a firm grip, looked them in the eye, and with a confident voice said, "Do you have any employment opportunities?" Instantly, the hiring manager would be interested.

Then, when the hiring manager asks them, "What hours would you be available?" and they reply with a quick, "I'm available any hours. I'll start right now. I'll do whatever it takes. I'll mop the floor. I'll clean the toilets. I'll clean the tables. Whatever you ask me to do, I'll do, and I'll be here on time every day, when I'm scheduled," they would have a job before they left. Some might start that day.

Those are the types of skills that I teach the boys every Tuesday. I teach them the rules of society, the things that most people are taught by their parents. I teach them interview skills and how to land a job. I teach them manners that get them noticed and accepted in society (just like Uncle Bobby taught me). I show them discipline and work ethic and the "don't stop" spirit that my mom instilled in me—and what that attitude got me. And I show them how to hustle the way my dad demonstrated for me, except legally.

Some other lessons I teach the boys each week:

Don't live check to check. I explain to them how to save money, how to plan ahead, and how to budget properly. It's simple to do, but no one has ever told them this, or how to not spend all their paycheck in a day.

Don't use check cashing stores. If you go to the check cashing places, they charge you 1 percent. If you've got $400 and someone takes $4, that hurts. That's a meal.

I tell them about banks. I teach these kids how to go open a checking account at a real bank. Those accounts are free. If you have a check, walk in and tell them, "I'd like to open a checking account." They will help you. But again, if all you know is the check cashing place by the liquor store, then that's where you're going to go.

I explain how to dress. Many grumble about having to wear nice slacks and a shirt and tie during an interview. They say they don't want a dress code; they feel like sellouts doing that.

I tell them, "Wait a minute. If I go to the hood, depending on what neighborhood I'm in, I may not be able to wear red or blue colors, right?" They nod in agreement, saying, "Yes, that's right, Mr. McCormick."

"That right there is a dress code. In corporate America, people are expected to dress according to their code, just like on the streets. Corporations have colors, too. The corporate world reps its hood just like the Crips and Bloods, but they do it with coats and ties, not guns and bandanas. And if you don't wear the corporate colors, you don't get shot; you just don't get a job. You get it now?"

When I explain it that way, they get it.

I teach them how to speak. There's a certain way people talk in business, and they complain about it and say it sounds weird. They say it's "talking white."

Well, there's a certain way people talk on the street, too. They have their own lingo and shorthand. You just have to learn the phrases and how to say them to fit in, just like you do to sit in a boardroom. In the hood, everyone knows that a trap house is a crack house; it's where a drug dealer makes money. In the boardroom, everyone knows what an EBITDA means. It stands for earnings before interest, tax, depreciation, and amortization.

The point is, I show them that every place has its own language, and you have to learn it to succeed in that environment.

I teach the boys about their body language, like how to shake hands. In the hood, people have fifteen-minute, elaborate handshakes they use when they meet someone. When you walk into a meeting in a conference room, there's a certain way you shake hands, too, with a firm grip, a smile on your face, and constant eye contact.

Once I explain the world of business to them in this manner, they get it. They start to see that Scarface was kind of right—the world is a ghetto. Every hood has its colors, its codes, and its slang. You just have to know where and how to look to see how the world and its rules work.

Once I explain the world of business to them in this language, they don't complain anymore. They start to map what they know about their world onto the business world, and it makes sense to them. They start to see the game and how they can play it well.

It's not foreign anymore. They just need a translator who speaks both languages.

* * *

One day, I asked the superintendent of the house if we could arrange a field trip.

Confused, he asked me, "What do you mean?"

I explained, "I'd love to bring the boys to my office to show them what one looks like, to show them computers and desks."

This was when I was still at Headspring. The superintendent agreed. So on a Saturday, I brought the kids to the office. I walked them through the halls and into the massive training room that housed two huge drop-down screens. I hooked up two PlayStations to the screens, ordered pizzas (for delivery), and let the boys play Madden football. They played and ate slices of cheese and pepperoni. They walked around and looked at the chairs and desks, the computers and the phones, and the pods that the Headspring team used. I let them have their pick of sodas and juices from a cooler branded with the company logo. They walked around, and I watched their faces and listened to their conversations.

"Have any of you ever been in an office?" I asked them. "No," everyone replied. *Of course they hadn't.* Office buildings don't exist in their world in the hood.

I figured the boys would be the most excited for the pizza and video games—what teenage boy wouldn't? Sure, they enjoyed those things, but that wasn't what they talked in awe about the most.

They were most obsessed with our restrooms, which had

wooden doors. The boys couldn't stop talking about how nice the restrooms were.

Anyone in the middle or upper class may find this funny. Who thinks twice about restrooms? And while the Head-spring restroom was nice, I'd been in fancier ones. But to those boys, restrooms with wooden doors belonged in a palace.

They didn't even know that bathrooms with wooden doors existed. They didn't know what they didn't know.

* * *

I didn't create society; I just learned its rules and I made them work for me. That's it. It's no different than playing a game of Monopoly. That's all any of us have to do to succeed in life. No matter where you are, if you can learn the rules of the game, you can make the game work for you. You can create your own opportunities.

Whether you're in the boardroom or on the street, there are rules. Most of the rules are the same, just with variations depending on the environment.

Too many kids (and people of all ages) are trapped, unable to live fulfilling lives because they don't know what they don't know. A kid born into a bad socioeconomic position grows up believing he has only three options for making money: become a drug dealer, a rapper, or an athlete. These are the only people they see and can identify with.

They don't see people like me, the people who have come from their background who got out. They don't see people like me walk into a halfway house, start speaking their language, trade the same horror stories of childhood, and then move into an executive board meeting and be just as at home there.

Regardless of your views on President Obama (and I won't disclose mine here), because he was elected, at least children of color can now say, "Wow, OK. Now a person of color can be president of the United States."

Being president of the United States is impossible to most kids (of any color), but having my job is not. There are lots of companies to run and to start.

People, especially kids, need to know what is achievable out there. They need to know what they can accomplish in their lives. They need to see that others have made it. And they need a map to get there.

These kids need to know that another path out of the hood is possible, but they need to see the path and some examples before they will take it.

If no one shows them how to shake hands, how to interact in the business world, how to speak respectfully by saying, "Thank you," and, "Yes, sir," then they don't know basic skills. If they don't know basic skills, they don't know the rules of how society works. If they don't know the rules of how society works, they can't play the game.

And if they can't play the game, they can't get out of the trap.

* * *

Before I can see the boys at the halfway house, I have to sign in and pick up my badge from the front desk. The kids can come only so far to the front desk; there's a hallway that separates us. Without fail, every week as I'm checking in, the boys line up along the wall waiting for me. Some start shouting my name, too excited to hold back.

"Mr. McCormick! Mr. McCormick!" they yell, trying to get my attention. "I got a job! I got a job!" they'll shout with broad grins.

They're thrilled and proud of their accomplishment—as they should be. And they want to share the great news with me, just like I once waited to show Uncle Bobby my report card. These kids need someone to be proud of them. I'm proud of them. They're putting the skills I teach them to use, and they're getting results.

I equip these kids with my lessons and encourage them, and then they leave and go out into the world. And the skills keep giving back. I get texts from them telling me things like, "Hey, Mr. McCormick, I was able to buy my son diapers. And I still have my job. Been there two years now, and I got a bunch of raises."

That's so incredible. Three years ago, that kid didn't believe he could have a better life, and now he's a productive member of society, a father, and he's proud of himself.

It chokes me up when I think about these kids and how teaching them the rules of society can make such a huge difference in their lives.

It makes me so happy to see them get jobs and to know that maybe they have a chance to rise from the streets, to make an honest living for themselves.

Many of the kids I've mentored have jobs. Some are assistant managers and moving up in the world. Lots are now out of the system for good and taking care of their own kids, being the fathers they never had. Two kids whom I've been mentoring for two years not only graduated high school, but they're also now enrolled in junior college.

Every year, I get a certificate thanking me for mentoring

these boys. For all my accomplishments and accolades, for all my successes, this one certificate is one of my most prized possessions and recognitions. It's greater than any college degree or MBA I could ever receive.

Quite honestly, a big part of this is giving back where I never got. It is fulfilling to be the man to these kids whom I never had in my life.

As proud as I am for these kids and as fulfilled as I feel for playing a role in their lives, I also shake my head in disappointment at our society for failing to teach them the rules of the game.

I don't believe that anyone wants to be poor. No one wants to stay in the hood. Most people just don't know what to do to rise. And they're afraid to try because they're afraid to fail, so they stay where they are.

We're all going to come across roadblocks in our lives. We're all going to come up against a brick wall. When this happens, what will you do? Will you go left or right to get around it? Will you climb over the top? Will you go straight through? Or will you let the wall turn you around or stop you in your tracks?

If you know what to do and you still stay where you are,

that responsibility is on you. But if you literally don't know what to do, then who is to blame?

And in fact, instead of finding whom to blame, how can we remove that roadblock? If the only roadblock is information, then isn't that easily solved?

I truly believe that whatever it is that you want to achieve, you can attain. I'm not sure we'll see an end to racism in this country, but I do believe the scales are more balanced than they've ever been. Anyone can achieve the American dream. You just have to be willing to work hard and sacrifice to do it, and you have to understand the game you are playing so you can play it well.

The fourth option is real. I did it, and I want to teach these kids how to do it, too.

GET THERE

I figured out a way to get there. I crossed my finish line.

I've shared my story because I want people to use it to see that it's possible to attain what they want. I've shared my story because I want to show everyone, especially kids who came from where I came from, that they can get out.

It's possible to overcome the obstacles in their way and achieve success.

I'm not sure what to do after this book. Of course, I will continue to mentor young kids in the Texas juvenile system. Those kids are me, and even though I can't go back and save myself, I can help those kids by giving them what I never got.

But I would like to do more. There are so many more kids to help and so many ways to help them. I want to end the book by putting out a call and seeing what happens:

If you are a young kid who read this book, if you want to know more, if you might want to have me mentor you and help you succeed, too, send me an email at jevon@ scribemedia.com.

I do read that email and I will respond. I will try my best to help you.

If you think you can help mentor young kids, email me.

If you have some ideas on how to help more kids, email me.

Basically, if you're as motivated as I am to help as many of these kids as possible to get where I got (or further), send me an email:

jevon@scribemedia.com

I can't make any promises as to what will happen.

I don't know how many people this book will reach.

I do know there are a lot of kids who can use help. If there are enough people who can help them, maybe we can create some real change.

Maybe together, we can create a world where everybody gets there.

Acknowledgments

———

WRITING A BOOK IS HARDER THAN I THOUGHT AND MORE rewarding than I could have ever imagined. None of this would have been possible without my best friend, Bishop. He was the first friend I made when I moved to San Antonio. He stood by me during every struggle and all my successes. That is true friendship.

I'm eternally grateful to my Uncle Bobby, who took in an extra mouth to feed when he didn't have to. He taught me discipline, tough love, manners, respect, and so much more that has helped me succeed in life. I truly have no idea where I'd be if he hadn't given me a roof over my head or become the father figure whom I desperately needed at that age.

To Mr. Gentry, who took a chance on a twenty-three-year-old kid and let him run his offices in Portland, Oregon. He never saw my age, my race, or my lack of formal education. He just saw a kid hungry to learn, hungry to grow, and hungry to succeed in business. He never stopped me; he only encouraged me.

Although this period of my life was filled with many ups and downs, my time in the mortgage industry was worth it. My time in the industry wouldn't have been possible without Guy Stidham, who taught me the honest mortgage game.

A very special thanks to Dustin Wells, who brought me on as the lowest-paid employee at Headspring and then allowed me to rise through the ranks to become president of the company. Thank you for introducing me to company culture.

Writing a book about the story of your life is a surreal process. I'm forever indebted to Tucker Max, Mark Chait, and Amanda Ibey for their editorial help, keen insight, and ongoing support in bringing my stories to life. It is because of their efforts and encouragement that I have a legacy to pass on to my family where one didn't exist before.

To everyone in the Scribe Tribe, who enable me to be the CEO of a company I'm honored to be a part of. Thank you for letting me serve, for being a part of our amazing company, and for showing up every day and helping more authors turn their ideas into books.

To my family:

To my stepfather, EJ, thank you for taking care of my mom, and for your guidance through the years.

To Aunt Jean: thank you for always being the person I could turn to during those dark and desperate years. You sustained me in ways that I never knew I needed.

To my little brother, Mario, and sisters, Rachel and Kristin: so thankful to have you back in my life. Thank you all for letting me know that you had nothing but great memories of me.

Finally, to all those who have been a part of my getting there: Jennifer Jackson, Kay Oder, Sharon Slonaker, Julie Fisher, Kathy Chesner, and Brother Smith (RIP). To the original Headspring team: Kevin Hurwitz, Jimmy Bogard, Mahendra Mavani, Pedro Reyes, Eric Sollenberger, Glenn Burnside, Justin Pope, Sharon Cechelli, and Anne Epstein.

About the Author

————

JEVON McCORMICK is currently the President and CEO of Scribe Media (formerly Book In A Box). Previously, he was the President of Headspring Software. He lives in Austin, Texas, with his wife, Megan, and their four children.

He can be reached at jevon@scribemedia.com.